W9-CHR-370

HEROES AND LEGENDS

KING ARTHUR

BY DANIEL MERSEY

ILLUSTRATED BY ALAN LATHWELL

ROSEN
PUBLISHING

NEW YORK

Published in 2015 by The Rosen Publishing Group, Inc.
29 East 21st Street, New York, NY 10010

First Edition

Library of Congress Cataloging-in-Publication Data

Mersey, Daniel.
King Arthur/Daniel Mersey.
    pages cm. — (Heroes and legends)
Originally published: Oxford: Osprey Publishing, 2013.
Includes bibliographical references and index.
ISBN 978-1-4777-8135-7 (library bound)
1. Arthur, King—Juvenile literature. 2. Great Britain—History—To 1066—Juvenile literature.
3. Britons—Kings and rulers—Folklore—Juvenile literature. I. Title.
DA152.5.A7M46 2015
942.01'4—dc23
                                                                                            2014020516

Manufactured in the United States of America

CONTENTS

INTRODUCTION

Arthur, the famous "once and future king of the Britons," is the most enduring hero of Western European literature. He features in many popular tales of bravery and adventure recorded over many centuries, but no definitive story of his legend exists.

Instead, Arthurian legend has two distinct strands of development: Arthur as a Dark Ages hero of Wales and the Celtic lands, and Arthur as a chivalrous medieval king whose fame spread across Europe between the twelfth and fifteenth centuries.

The Celtic Arthur had many forms: He was sometimes a brave warrior, sometimes a trickster or tyrant. But in later medieval Europe, Arthur was considered one of the Nine Worthies alongside historical figures such as Alexander the Great and Charlemagne: He was a noble and powerful king ruling from the majestic castle of Camelot. In the space of two hundred years, Arthur was propelled from regional folk hero of the Celts to the embodiment of European chivalry.

After the medieval period, Arthur languished somewhat in popular imagination, but memories of his great empire were revived in the Victorian era with authors such as Alfred Lord Tennyson contributing to his legend. He has remained popular in fiction ever since and has also fared well in Hollywood: Perhaps the finest retelling of Arthurian legend in film came in 1981 with John Boorman's *Excalibur*, a breathtaking compression of Arthur's world into 135 minutes of cinema.

Arguably, a third Arthur exists as an historical leader in the fifth or sixth centuries. Arthur is both a curse and a blessing to this period. Many pages have been devoted to the ongoing search to identify a "real" Arthur, but this single-minded quest too often crushes the rest of the period's fascinating if uncertain history.

Accounting for the entire legend of a hero so complex as Arthur, recited and reinvented time and again over at least one thousand years, is impossible in a book of this length. Therefore this account focuses on crucial plot development and canonical stories, alongside some less well-known tales offering glimpses of the "original" heroic Arthur.

The Celtic tales in this book are not direct translations of the surviving texts, preferring instead to convey the spirit of early Arthurian storytelling; academic translations may be found in some of the titles referenced in this

Actor Nigel Terry played Arthur in John Boorman's movie *Excalibur*. Released in 1981, it remains the most evocative retelling of Arthurian legend on film. (Corbis Images)

book. Personal names and locations have varied in their spelling over time, but these are standardized where possible within each chapter; checking the original source material will highlight variations from the names shown in this book.

THE MEDIEVAL ARTHUR

The most famous tales of Arthur were told first by English and French writers between the twelfth and fifteenth centuries and even today are little changed from the originals. The best-known Arthurian author of any period is England's Sir Thomas Malory, whose fifteenth-century tales are considered to be a milestone in the retelling of Arthur's legend and in the development of printing and publishing; Malory's work has influenced almost all writers of Arthurian literature who came after him.

However, Malory was not the first medieval writer to weave these tales about this mysterious yet magnificent king, as he followed a rich tradition of Arthurian story telling that had built up in the centuries before his lifetime. The father of this earlier medieval tradition is considered to be Geoffrey of Monmouth.

English and French medieval tales of Arthur and his knights generally fall into one of two camps: stories learned from traditional Celtic originals and restyled to appeal to their new audience, and stories invented to demonstrate the courtly behaviours of chivalric English and French medieval knights, which are more loosely linked to their Arthurian setting. Eventually both strands of the legend merged in the works of Malory.

Geoffrey of Monmouth: The History of the Kings of Britain

The earliest surviving English or French account of Arthur running to any substantial length is Geoffrey of Monmouth's *The History of the Kings of Britain* (*Historia regum Britanniae*), completed c. 1136. Geoffrey's tale of Arthur introduced many of the plots and ideas that became the backbone of Arthurian legend. However, his Arthur is not quite the chivalric champion of the later medieval period, instead reflecting a curious combination of Dark Ages warlord and contemporary twelfth-century king. Geoffrey's narrative was the first popular story of Arthur, but also differed in many ways to the later, more familiar tales.

Although Geoffrey was the first medieval writer to promote Arthur in detail, two Anglo-Norman writers mentioned Arthur in passing at an earlier date. William of Malmesbury included a passing reference to Arthur in his *Deeds of the English Kings (Gesta regum Anglorum)*, which was completed in 1125, noting that the Britons recited oral traditions of Arthur and describing their stories as nonsense. Four years after William completed his work and a few years before Geoffrey of Monmouth, Henry of Huntingdon listed 12 battles that Arthur had fought and won in *The History of the English People (Historia Anglorum)*. Henry's list was taken from a British account of Arthur written a couple of hundred years earlier. The original Celtic versions of both of these stories are covered in the next chapter.

Arthur's victory at Bedegraine, a battle fought to prove his right to rule as the Pendragon. From the *Story of Merlin*, c. 1280–90. (Bibliotheque Nationale, Paris, France / The Bridgeman Art Library)

Geoffrey's work *The History of the Kings of Britain* begins with Albion as an isolated, magical land inhabited by giants. Around 1200 BCE, Brutus of Troy arrived on the shores of Albion. Brutus and his followers fought the giants and conquered the island, renaming it Britain in honour of their leader; henceforth the inhabitants were known as Britons. Geoffrey describes the reigns of around 75 other kings, most of them seemingly coming from the depths of his own imagination rather than any historical source.

Despite Geoffrey's fictitious vision of British history, it is possible that there were elements of truth in his writing. Some of his immediately pre-Roman and Roman history bears some relation to that recorded elsewhere, although there is no consistency or prolonged accuracy in Geoffrey's work. Geoffrey claimed that Walter, Archdeacon of Oxford, presented him with an ancient book written in the British language listing everything he had included in his own work. If Geoffrey did indeed have such a major source, it has long since been lost, and even some of his contemporaries branded him a liar.

The part of Geoffrey's *History* that tells us of Arthur occurs after the end of Roman dominance. This period occurred in Geoffrey's *History* roughly from the mid-fifth to mid-sixth centuries, with his Arthur coming to the throne around 490 (the actual date is not stated by Geoffrey) and dying in 542.

Arthur: The Boar of Cornwall

After the Romans left Britain, civil war and barbaric Pictish and Irish raiders plagued the island. British nobles vied for power: one group was led by Aurelius Ambrosius and his brother Uther, and the other by Great Lord Vortigern and his mercenary Saxon allies. Vortigern's Saxons rebelled and took control of the lowlands, although the boy wizard Merlin prophesized an eventual British victory symbolized by two dragons – red for the Britons, white for the Saxons – fighting in a magical cave beneath Snowdonia.

Ambrosius and Uther deposed Vortigern and put his Saxon generals Hengist and Horsa to death. Ambrosius was crowned Pendragon, the Chief Dragon of Britain, and set about restoring the island to its former glory. But he was soon poisoned by Vortigern's son Pascent and was succeeded by Uther. Uther successfully fought against the remaining rebellious Britons and Saxons in a lengthy war, but also fell victim to a poisoner.

Uther was succeeded as Pendragon by his son Arthur, a fifteen-year-old boy who was crowned at Silchester. Arthur had been conceived with the help of magic at Tintagel by Uther and the Duke of Cornwall's wife Igraine; Merlin altered Uther's appearance to that of the rebellious duke, allowing him to sleep with Igraine. The duke was slain and Igraine became Uther's queen.

Arthur – the Boar of Cornwall – immediately embarked upon a military campaign against the hated Saxons. Aided by the Picts from the north and the Irish from the west, the Saxons put up a strong fight but Arthur defeated them in three battles and the Saxons surrendered, promising to leave Britain. The Saxons broke their treaty but Arthur won a decisive victory at Bath and the Saxons never again proved a threat during Arthur's reign.

In battle, Arthur wielded a sword named Caliburn, forged on the enchanted Isle of Avalon; he also carried a shield emblazoned with the image of the Virgin Mary to demonstrate his Christian belief, and wore a golden helmet with the crest of a dragon to symbolize his title of Pendragon.

Once he had crushed the Saxon threat, Arthur turned his attention to the Picts and Irish. Arthur destroyed their alliance and was only prevented from wiping every last enemy warrior out by the intervention of their bishops. Victory complete against the enemies of the Britons, Arthur set about restoring the stability of Britain's government and churches. Arthur ruled fairly and married a woman of Roman descent named Guinevere.

With the safety of Britain restored, Arthur expanded his empire into Ireland and Iceland. He then looked to challenge the might of the Roman Empire by sending an army into Roman Gaul. When Arthur's Britons and the Roman army met in battle, the Roman leader managed to run Arthur's

Uther Pendragon by Howard Pyle. Uther was Arthur's father and ruled before him as a great warrior king of the Britons and the scourge of the Saxons.

horse through with a lance before the British king split the Roman's head in two with a mighty blow from Caliburn. The Roman army immediately surrendered, and Arthur subdued the rest of Gaul. Arthur applied the same sense of justice and fair rule to his foreign subjects as he did within Britain.

Arthur held court at Caerleon on the banks of the River Usk in south Wales. He hosted a tournament for his knights to demonstrate their battle skills and invited the many leaders who now owed him homage. An envoy arrived at Arthur's court, bringing a message from Rome condemning the king's behaviour. The message stated that Arthur had not paid the tribute that Rome was accustomed to receiving from the Britons, and that Arthur had unfairly seized Roman land in Gaul. If the British king did not submit, a state of war and a Roman reconquest of Arthur's lands would follow.

Arthur meets the giant roasting a pig on a spit, from a fourteenth-century verse chronicle of *Roman de Brut*. Geoffrey of Monmouth and the ever-bloodthirsty Layamon both retold this earlier tale of Arthur's giant-slaying prowess. (British Library, London, UK / The Bridgeman Art Library)

With that, Arthur's army set out to campaign against Rome once more. Arthur led his army in person, leaving his nephew Mordred and his wife Guinevere to rule Britain jointly in his absence. On the brief sea journey crossing to the continent, Arthur dreamed of a dragon fighting a bear; the dragon was victorious, and Arthur's warriors interpreted this vision with Arthur as the dragon and the bear as either the Roman emperor or a fabulous beast that their king would defeat in battle.

As Arthur waited for his allied kings to join him in Gaul, it was reported that a huge giant was terrorizing the region, having arrived from Spain. Helena, the niece of the local duke, had been snatched by the giant and taken to the top of the Mont Saint Michel. Arthur was told that Gallic knights had tried in vain to fight the giant, but all had either died quickly or had been captured and eaten while they were still alive. To inspire confidence in his men for the coming conflict against Rome, Arthur decided to take his knights Bedivere and Kay with him to challenge the giant. The three heroes were too late to save Helena, but Arthur killed the giant and Bedivere took its head back to the British camp so that everyone could witness Arthur's feat of arms. Perhaps the giant had been the bear of Arthur's dream.

Arthur's nephew, Gawain, fought the first battle against Rome, leading six thousand warriors against a Roman force of ten thousand. Other battles followed, and at Saussy the two main armies drew up against one another. The Britons fell in great numbers before pushing the Romans back. Arthur was in the thick of battle, once again wielding Caliburn with great prowess, and the Roman host broke and ran from the British army.

Arthur stayed on the continent during the winter, and when summer arrived he prepared his army to cross the Alps and head directly for Rome to confront the emperor. He had defeated the empire's greatest army, and now intended to claim the city of Rome as part of his kingdom; by doing so, all of Europe would be ruled by the king of the Britons. He had already started into the mountain passes when news arrived that Mordred – the nephew he had left to rule Britain in his absence – had taken the crown of Britain for himself. What was more, Arthur's wife Guinevere had sided with Mordred. Arthur turned his army around and headed back for Britain to retake his kingdom.

Mordred had made a pact with the old enemies of the Britons: Saxons, Irish, and Picts. Arthur arrived back in Britain to be confronted by an army of some eighty thousand hostile warriors, whom Arthur drove back from his landing site at Richborough despite the death of his loyal nephew Gawain.

A bloody campaign to return Arthur to his throne began, and Guinevere fled to York to become a nun. Arthur cornered Mordred's army in Cornwall at Camelford, where the two armies clashed once more. Mordred was slain and his army was utterly defeated. Arthur himself was mortally wounded and was carried away to have his wounds tended on the Isle of Avalon, the enchanted island where his sword Caliburn had been forged. He was succeeded by Constantine of Cornwall.

ARTHUR SLAYS A GIANT

This plate depicts Arthur fighting the giant of Mont Saint Michel in Brittany. The story is told in Geoffrey of Monmouth's *The History of the Kings of Britain* (*Historia Regnum Britannae*), but is almost certainly based on an older tale about Arthur as his original Celtic companions Kay and Bedivere are present.

Arthur's army landed in Brittany, ready to fight against the armies of Rome. Arthur was approached by his Breton ally Hoel: Hoel's knights had been defeated by a marauding giant based on Mont Saint Michel and the giant had now taken his niece Helena. Approaching the giant's camp at night, Arthur rushed to fight the giant by himself (as described in Lewis Thorpe's 1966 translation):

At that moment the inhuman monster was standing by his fire. His face was smeared with the clotted blood of a number of pigs at which he had been gnawing. He had swallowed bits of them while he was roasting the rest over the live embers on the spits to which he had fixed them. The moment he saw the newcomers, nothing then being farther from his thoughts, he rushed to snatch up his club, which two young men would have found difficulty in lifting off the ground.

Although battered by the club, Arthur killed the giant and Bedivere beheaded it, taking this back to the British army's camp to demonstrate Arthur's great victory. Sadly for Hoel, Helena had already been slain by the giant.

The Legend Evolves

Shortly after Geoffrey of Monmouth came the poet Wace. He was a native of the Channel Island of Jersey and was a prolific writer. In 1155, he completed a version of Geoffrey's work, adapted into French verse, and dedicated it to Eleanor, queen of Henry II of England.

Wace called his Arthurian work the *Romance of Brutus* (*Roman de Brut*) and made two important changes to Geoffrey's work. He introduced Arthur's famous Round Table to the tale, which had no head or foot so that all who sat at it were equal. The second important alteration that Wace made to Geoffrey's work was at the end of Arthur's reign. Wace predicted that Arthur would return from Avalon when the time was right, and that the king and his knights had not died but were sleeping. Wace popularized the idea of Arthur as "the once and future king," although this inclusion may well have been based on existing British or Breton folklore.

Chrétien de Troyes was the most important author of the French school of Arthurian romance, which focussed on love and chivalric adventure. The plot of an Arthurian romance usually concentrated on the deeds of one knight: this knight would undertake various adventures – sometimes supernatural or fantastic – in order to make a triumphant return to court. Chrétien's contributions were an important milestone in the medieval understanding of how chivalry should be defined and attained. He lived in the latter half of the twelfth century, and all five of his Arthurian romances are broadly attributed to the period 1170–90: *Erec and Enide* (*Erec et Enide*); *Cligés*; *Lancelot, the Knight of the Cart* (*Lancelot, le Chevalier de la Charrette*); *Yvain, the Knight of the Lion* (*Yvain, le Chevalier au Lion*); and *Perceval, the Story of the Grail* (*Perceval, le Conte du Graal*). The last of these – featuring the Holy Grail – was unfinished by Chrétien, probably due to his death, but several other writers added their own endings and these are known as the *Grail Continuations*.

Shortly after Chrétien de Troyes came Layamon, who was an English priest from the Welsh borders. At some point around the end of the twelfth century or beginning of the thirteenth century

Perceval was the original hero of the Grail Quest, but in later tales Galahad replaced him as the central character. From *La Prophetie de Merlin*, 1875. (Author's Collection)

he translated Wace's *Romance of Brutus*, composing this alliterative verse in English rather than Latin or French. As such, Layamon should be credited with the first Arthurian tales produced in English. Layamon introduced both the name of Arthur's sword as Excalibur and the contest of the sword in the stone to determine Arthur's right to rule. Layamon's Arthur was a man of action and adventure: As with Geoffrey of Monmouth's king, blood and violence ruled in Layamon's recital, setting it apart from the development of

Arthurian romance on the continent. His Arthur was blessed at birth by elves, and the wounds Arthur received at Camlann were treated by magic on the Isle of Avalon by the elf queen Argante.

The Vulgate Cycle was the next significant development in Arthurian literature. This was a sprawling collection of early thirteenth-century romance prose composed by a group of French monks. There are five main stories within this ambitious cycle: *The History of the Holy Grail* (*Estoire del Saint Grail*), *Merlin* (*Estoire de Merlin*), *Lancelot* (*Lancelot Proper*), *The Quest of the Holy Grail* (*Queste del Saint Graal*), and *The Death of Arthur* (*Mort Artu*). These stories had a huge influence on later Arthurian authors and presented some of the canonical plot lines of popular Arthurian literature, including the introduction of Lancelot as a major character.

Geoffrey of Monmouth's Arthur was simply a great king, strong in battle, and Chrétien de Troye's Arthurian tales emphasized courtly behaviour and romance, but the Vulgate Cycle emphasized Christianity and religion in the world of Arthur. Very quickly, the Grail Quest became a central theme of the legend.

The Vulgate Cycle was not the first Arthurian mention of the Holy Grail – Chrétien de Troyes's final, uncompleted poem did so – but these tales were the first to go into any great detail about this revered religious artefact. The

A CAST OF THOUSANDS

Chrétien de Troyes and later writers frequently used characters other than Arthur as the hero of their stories. Arthur often provided a start and end to the tale, but the action focussed on the deeds of Arthur's knights or enemies. Following are some of the most significant characters from medieval Arthurian legend:

Bedivere: A loyal knight who returned Excalibur to a lake as Arthur lay mortally wounded.

Ector: Arthur's foster father, entrusted by Merlin to bring the boy up honorably.

Galahad: The embodiment of chivalry, who succeeded in the Grail Quest.

Gawain: Arthur's loyal nephew and champion, eventually slain by Lancelot.

Guinevere: Arthur's wife, whose affair with Lancelot led to Arthur's demise.

Igraine: Arthur's mother who was magically deceived by Merlin into sleeping with Uther.

Kay: Arthur's foster brother, rash and sharp-tongued but also loyal.

Lancelot: The finest warrior at Camelot, who fell in love with Guinevere.

Merlin: Wise counsellor, prophet, and supernatural wizard whose story interweaves with that of Uther and Arthur.

Mordred: Arthur's nephew and greatest enemy, the eventual usurper of the king.

Morgan: Arthur's half-sister and the enchantress of Avalon; in early tales she healed Arthur, but in the Vulgate Cycle she became an enemy.

Morgause: Arthur's half-sister who slept with him and conceived Mordred; also the mother of Gawain and several other knights.

Perceval: Good-natured and innocent, Perceval was the original hero of the Grail Quest, eventually supplanted by Galahad.

Uther: Arthur's father and Pendragon before him, sometimes assisted by Merlin.

Viviane: The Lady of the Lake, a mysterious water nymph who was the guardian of Excalibur and the mentor of Lancelot.

The Rescue of Queen Guinevere by Sir Lancelot by William Hatherell. (The Bridgeman Art Library)

Holy Grail was never fully described in the earliest stories, but most authors depict it as the silver cup that Joseph of Arimathea used to collect blood from Jesus' wounds. Robert de Boron, a Burgundian poet, was the first explicitly to depict the Holy Grail as a holy relic associated with the Crucifixion, rather than as a magical object. He composed three Arthurian romances at the end of the twelfth or the start of the thirteenth century: *The Chronicle of the History of the Grail* (*Joseph d'Arimathe*), *Merlin*, and *Perceval*.

Romances in English, both in verse and prose, sprang up from the thirteenth century onwards, including *Sir Launfal* written around 1350 by Thomas Chestre, *Ywain and Gawain* also written in the mid-fourteenth century, and two late fourteenth-century tales: *Sir Gawain and the Green Knight*, and *The Adventures of Arthur* (*The Awntyrs off Arthure*). These English texts are typically reduced versions of earlier French texts, adapted from the original tales to read as action-packed adventure stories.

Continental writers contributed their own tales of the Knights of the Round Table, including the Germans Hartmann von Aue and Wolfram von Eschenbach, who created *Iwein* and *Parzival* respectively (adapted from the French tales of *Yvain* and *Perceval*). In Ireland, a translation of the Vulgate Cycle's *The Quest of the Holy Grail* was created in the fourteenth or fifteenth centuries, and Scottish poets adapted the stories of Lancelot and Gawain for their own audiences. Despite their own strong traditions of Arthur, even Welsh writers adapted English and French tales to a Celtic setting more familiar to their audience.

Sir Thomas Malory: The Death of Arthur

Malory completed *The Death of Arthur* (*Le Morte d'Arthur*) in 1469 or 1470, but the most famous date associated with his Arthurian masterpiece is 1485, when William Caxton printed the text as a book. Several people named Thomas Malory have been identified as potential authors of *The Death of Arthur*, but Sir Thomas Malory of Newbold Revel in Warwickshire is the most likely candidate. It seems he wrote this tale of chivalry and adventure when he was in prison – he describes himself as a "knight-prisoner" – and that he died around 1471.

Contrary to the title of the piece, *The Death of Arthur* recounts Arthur's reign in its entirety, not just the ending. The story begins with the conception of Arthur, son of Uther Pendragon, and ends with the death of Lancelot and the crowning of Constantine as Arthur's successor. Many of the deeds of Arthur's knights and the quest for the Holy Grail are retold, but throughout the middle section of *The Death of Arthur* the king takes a back seat, often appearing only at the beginning and end of each tale. The deeds of Lancelot are dealt with in detail, and an epic battle between Arthur and Mordred dominates the end of the book, with the king once again becoming the focal point of the story.

Most modern adaptations of Arthurian legend are based on Malory's fifteenth-century writings. It is fitting that his tales should remain so well known, as they are very much the culmination of earlier English and French medieval tradition consolidated into one unified cycle.

Arthur: High King of Camelot

The High King Uther Pendragon – the Chief Dragon of Britain – was a strong ruler and necessarily so. He not only had to contend with raids from barbaric Irish, Picts and Saxons, but also with rebellious Britons. With the aid of a sizeable army and an ancient, wise counsellor named Merlin, Uther brought peace across the lands of Britain, except for the island's south-western tip, where the Duke of Cornwall rebelled against him.

Uther marched his army to besiege the insubordinate duke in his castle at Tintagel. During the siege Uther's lust for the duke's wife, Igraine, overtook his need for victory, and he summoned Merlin to help him. Merlin agreed to aid Uther in return for a gift. Uther eagerly agreed.

Merlin urged Uther to drink a magical potion that altered Uther's appearance to mirror that of the rebellious duke. Uther, in the guise of the duke, entered the castle and slept with Igraine, who believed him to be her husband. The same night, the duke was slain by Uther's army and Tintagel's resistance crumbled. With Tintagel in the hands of Uther's men, the king confessed his true identity to Igraine, forcibly taking her hand in marriage. Following a prophecy from Merlin, a child was born to the new queen as a result of Uther's deception. Igraine's first and only act as a mother was to name the child Arthur, as Merlin claimed his gift from Uther, carrying the baby away into the hills of Wales.

Uther fell ill and the Saxons, Irish, and Picts returned to his kingdom. Returned to health by Merlin, Uther led his army against the enemies of Britain and won a great victory. During the battle, however, Uther was dealt a fatal blow and died three days after his triumphant return to London. The death of Uther was a prelude to greater disaster: The British nobles, no longer having to fight the barbarians whom Uther had decisively defeated, renewed their feuds and for more than a decade Briton fought Briton.

Merlin planned to restore peace, but he needed patience for his plan to fall into place. He foresaw great things for Arthur – even before the boy was conceived – and wished for him to grow into knighthood untainted by the pettiness of court life. He had taken the baby Arthur to Ector, a knight who lived deep in the Welsh hills. Ector had a son, Kay, who was only a few years older than Arthur and Ector brought them up together. Though he was not

MERLIN.TAKETH.THE. CHILD.ARTHVR.INTO. HIS.KEEPING.

Merlin taketh the child Arthur into his keeping by Aubrey Beardsley. (Author's Collection)

a rich knight, Ector instead showed them how an honorable knight should act. He taught them the folly of the power struggles within Britain, and drilled them well in preparation for knighthood.

Merlin and his confidant the archbishop of Canterbury realized that a new king could not be crowned by words alone, but, convinced that Arthur was Uther's rightful heir, they agreed on a course of action to bring the fifteen-year-old boy to the throne. Merlin's work done, he disappeared once more.

All of the British knights were summoned to London at Christmas, and informed by the archbishop that the strongest among them would be crowned High King. A great number of nobles descended upon London, ready for the chance to be crowned High King; Ector and his sons arrived out of curiosity. At London's great cathedral they saw a wonder to surpass any other: standing prominently in the cathedral's grounds was a great square stone, atop which was a steel anvil, and deep into that anvil a brilliant, shining sword had been driven. The knights gathered around, where they saw that the stone carried an inscription:

"Who so pulleth out the sword from this stone and anvil is the rightful and true-born High King of the Britons."

The foremost dukes pushed their way to the front, intent on wrenching the sword from its resting place. Many tried, but not one could move the sword. Disenchanted and humiliated, the dukes began to argue among themselves.

Acting on advice left by Merlin, the archbishop quickly announced that a tournament would be held on New Year's Day, and that the dukes should save their strength and anger for that. Ector and Kay, whose lowly rank had prevented them from attempting to remove the sword, retired to prepare for the tournament and Arthur readied himself to act as their squire.

As church bells rang in the New Year, knights and peasants alike flocked to the city. Having never attended such a grand tournament before, it was not surprising that Arthur forgot one crucial item. As he helped Kay into his armour shortly before his first joust, the pair of them realized that Kay did not have his sword. Arthur rushed off to find a replacement.

With so little time in which to find a sword, Arthur panicked. And then he remembered the sword in the stone, the only sword in London not already sitting in a knight's scabbard. The cathedral grounds were empty when Arthur arrived, and he strode up to the shimmering sword still lodged in the anvil on the stone and with no effort at all drew it. Arthur had drawn the sword: the sword of the rightful High King of Britain.

Arthur returned to Kay as fast as he could and thrust the brilliant sword into his brother's hand. Kay marvelled at the quality of the blade, and asked Arthur where he had found such a weapon; Arthur told him, and Kay turned to his father Ector and announced himself as the rightful heir to the throne.

Ector watched as Kay held the sword aloft, while Arthur stood close by regaining his breath after his desperate quest for a weapon. When Ector asked Kay if he had drawn the sword himself, Kay could no longer lie and announced that Arthur had done so. Ector led his sons back to the cathedral grounds, and asked Arthur to replace the sword into the anvil. He then asked Kay to remove the sword, but try as he might Kay could not manage to do so. Ector then asked Arthur to remove the sword, and the younger boy did so without the slightest effort. With that, both Ector and Kay fell to their knees and kissed the hand of the rightful High King of Britain.

This event had not gone unnoticed, for the archbishop had stood watching the trio by the stone, and Ector told him what had happened. He also told the archbishop that Merlin had brought Arthur to him as a baby, and entrusted him to his care. In turn, the archbishop told Ector, Kay and Arthur what Merlin had revealed to him: Arthur was the son of Uther Pendragon, and was indeed the rightful heir to the throne.

The archbishop sent word to the tournament that the new king of the Britons had been found, and an excited crowd gathered at the cathedral, from the noblest dukes to the commonest folk of London. They all wished to see their powerful new king and were astonished to see a boy pushed before them and announced as King Arthur. The archbishop told Arthur to replace the sword and draw it from the anvil once more. Arthur drew the sword three more times before the majority of the dukes believed what they were witnessing, and even then a number rode away angrily, declaring this to be a trick.

Some accepted what they saw; Arthur was knighted by Ulfius and Brastias, two of the greatest British dukes, and preparations were made for the coronation. On a bright January morning Arthur was crowned king and swore an oath to commoner and noble alike that he would be an honourable king until his dying day.

Arthur appointed a number of royal dignitaries with the help of Merlin, who had returned to see the boy's coronation. Kay was appointed steward, Ulfius was granted the role of chamberlain, and Brastias was given the task of defending the borderlands from Pictish, Irish, and Saxon armies.

Arthur asked Merlin what he should do next; he was painfully aware of his lack of regal knowledge. Merlin simply advised Arthur to head to the royal court of Camelot and take up his royal residence there.

Arthur followed Merlin's advice, and Kay set about organizing a great banquet for the new royal household. Among the nobles who had gathered at Camelot to pay their respects to the new king were six kings in their own right, including the powerful Lot of Orkney and Urien of Gore. But instead of feasting, the six kings declared that Arthur was a mere boy and not fit to rule. Their warriors laid siege to Camelot, and within days, Britain had lurched from a joyous coronation to the outbreak of war.

Arthur rode into battle against the six rebel kings, under the dragon banner of Uther Pendragon, and defeated them. Arthur excelled in the battle – even though this was his first – and further gained the respect of the knights and

The arming and departure of the knights by Edward Burne-Jones. Burne-Jones was an influential artist in the Victorian revival of Arthurian legend. (Birmingham Museums and Art Gallery / The Bridgeman Art Library)

dukes who fought for him. All six of Arthur's enemy leaders fled and regrouped, bringing with them five more rebel kings. Once more Arthur led his loyal knights into battle, this time on the banks of the River Humber, and once more the bravery of both him and his men won the day. Yet he could not have done so without the intervention of the loyal King Ban of Benwick, a colony of Britons on mainland Europe, who sent a large number of battle hardened knights to help his new High King. With the defeat of the rebel kings, and the sworn loyalty of those who fought for him in his first battle, Arthur and his trusted advisor Merlin continued to heal the wounds of Britain.

In a series of battles culminating with a great victory at Badon Hill near to Bath, Arthur's armies defeated the Saxons, the Irish, and the Picts. He gained the loyalty of these peoples' own kings, and as Arthur's power grew, and as his benevolent influence was seen to succeed, more British dukes rallied behind him, pledging the support of themselves and their allies. The boy king had regained the unity lost by the Britons so long before.

EXCALIBUR RISES

In a duel with Pellinore soon after he was crowned, Arthur broke the blade of the sword he drew from the stone to prove his kingship; after the duel, Merlin led Arthur to a nearby lake, where the magical Lady of the Lake – Viviane – emerged to gift Arthur his new sword: Excalibur.

This plate depicts Excalibur rising from the lake and Arthur seeing his new weapon for the very first time; this is one of the best-known scenes from Arthurian legend, but is often conflated with the story of the Sword in the Stone. The Sword in the Stone was a different weapon, sometimes named as Galatine or Sequence, and described by Malory as a "fair sword"; Arthur was already king when he received Excalibur from the Lady of the Lake.

The name Excalibur was first used in Layamon's bloodthirsty retelling of Wace's *Romance of Brutus*. By Malory's time the weapon's scabbard had taken on magical qualities of its own, with the wearer losing no blood regardless of his wounds. Geoffrey of Monmouth named Arthur's sword Caliburn ("steel"); this probably derived from the earlier Welsh tale of *Culhwch and Olwen* where Arthur's sword is named Caledfwlch ("hard cut"), which itself may have evolved from the magical Irish sword Caledbolg ("hard lightning") belonging to Fergus mac Roich. In *The Spoils of the Otherworld*, a sword

named "lightning slaughter" is used in battle, although this is seemingly not Arthur's weapon.

In the *Dream of Rhonabwy*, Arthur's sword is not named but is described:

> Cador of Cornwall stood up with Arthur's sword in his hand and the image of two golden serpents on the sword's hilt. When the sword was drawn from its scabbard, it was like seeing two flames of fire from the serpents' mouths. It was not easy for anyone to look at the sword because it was so terrifying.

Alfred Lord Tennyson described Excalibur as a very grand weapon in "The Passing of Arthur" (published in his *Idylls of the King* cycle between 1856 and 1885), although such decoration might be impractical in battle:

> There drew he forth the brand Excalibur,
> And o'er him, drawing it, the winter moon,
> Brightening the skirts of a long cloud, ran forth
> And sparkled keen with frost against the hilt:
> For all the haft twinkled with diamond sparks,
> Myriads of topaz-lights, and jacinth-work
> Of subtlest jewellery.

Faugh Sir! You smell of ye Kitchen

Gareth & Linet

Gareth & Linet by H. J. Ford. Gareth was a brother of Gawain who arrived at Camelot as a kitchen boy before escorting Linet on a quest to free her sister. (Author's Collection)

Even with the allegiance of his former enemies, Arthur still had much work to do to restore peace and justice to a land long used to anarchy, but each and every week saw more knights arriving at Camelot to serve their new king. Not only did Arthur restore peace to Britain, but he also conquered Rome by defeating the Emperor Lucius.

One day, word came to Arthur that a knight had set up camp in a nearby forest, questing after a miraculous beast. Offering to joust with any other passing knight, this stranger had bettered several of Camelot's warriors. Arthur rode out to meet this troublesome knight, accompanied by Merlin.

Arthur entered the camp and blew a horn hanging from a tree at the edge of the clearing. Upon hearing this sound, a huge knight appeared. The knight declared that he was hunting a magical beast and to prevent others from taking this quest from him, he was jousting with any knight who passed by. The knight then kicked his horse into a gallop towards Arthur. Arthur did the same, and the pair crashed their lances onto each other's shield. Unseated, Arthur struggled to his feet, and his opponent lunged towards him with a sword. The duel went on for a lengthy time – hours – until suddenly, Arthur's sword snapped in two whilst parrying a tremendous blow from his opponent. At that point, the huge knight fell to the ground with a snore.

Merlin had magicked Arthur's opponent into a deep sleep. This fearsome knight, he explained, was Pellinore, and he would be of great service to Arthur. Pellinore was chasing a strange creature known as the Questing Beast, with the head of a serpent, the body of a leopard, and the sound of baying hounds in its belly; Merlin believed the creature would never be captured, and that the pursuit was driving Pellinore slightly mad. Even so, as he was a good knight who would serve Arthur well, Merlin had magically ended the fight.

Arthur stood with his sword broken in two. The sword he had drawn from the stone was no more; his symbol of authority had been shattered. Merlin advised him to go to the edge of the lake that stood close by, and as Arthur did so the water in the middle of the lake began to ripple. A gleaming metal point emerged from beneath the lake's surface and a glorious sword emerged aloft in a maiden's hand. As the sword and arm stood proud, the lake was suddenly calm. Merlin suggested that Arthur should fetch his new sword and indicated a small rowing boat close by. Arthur pushed the boat out into the water, and rowed toward the sword. As he approached, he stared down into the water, and saw the shape of a beautiful woman. He clasped the sword's hilt and with this the arm and body gracefully slipped away, sinking into the depths of the lake. Merlin beckoned Arthur back to the shore.

As the astonished Arthur clambered out of the boat Merlin told him that he had just met the Lady of the Lake, a powerful enchantress who wished to acknowledge Arthur's kingship with this gift. Turning to the sword in Arthur's hand, Merlin explained that it was named Excalibur, and that it would bring the king many victories.

Early in his reign, Arthur and his half-sister Morgause – both unaware of their bloodline – conceived Mordred, who would later serve as one of Arthur's knights; foreseeing distant disaster from this union, Merlin advised Arthur to kill every newborn boy in the kingdom, but Mordred escaped.

Arthur fell in love with the noble Guinevere: she was the most beautiful woman Arthur had ever seen. Guinevere, Merlin pointed out, was an attractive and strong-minded woman, but whether she would make a suitable queen for the High King of Britain, he did not know; despite this Arthur asked for Guinevere's hand in marriage. Guinevere's father's wedding gift was a round table, beautifully crafted from very ancient wood, with 150 chairs seated around it. Its shape meant that no knight who took his place at a seat could be considered any closer to the head of the table than any other seated knight, and this symbolized democracy, piety, and equality between the High King, his dukes, and his knights. Arthur announced on his wedding night that he would form the Order of the Round Table.

The Order would be made up of the 150 most chivalrous and renowned knights in Britain, each of who swore to abide by Arthur's rule and act with the same judgement and honour as

Guinevere by Dante Gabriel Rossetti. Arthur's queen was described by Geoffrey of Monmouth as being of Roman blood and brought up by Cador of Cornwall; in later legend, she was the daughter of Leodegrance, who gave Arthur the Round Table as a wedding gift. (Author's Collection)

the king himself. Among the first to sit at the Round Table were Ector, Kay, Pellinore, Ulfius, Brastias, Gawain, and Lucas, all of whom had loyally served Arthur from the start of his reign. The Order was true to its word, and the kingdom flourished under the just rule of Arthur and the beautiful Guinevere.

The deeds of the Knights of the Round Table were many and varied. Each knight completed many brave and honorable tasks, bringing further glory to Arthur's realm. Among their number were many famous knights: Balin and Balan, the tragic brothers who killed each other in a duel without realizing whom they fought; Yvain, who befriended a lion after protecting it from a dragon's attack; Tristan, who loved King Mark's wife Isolde and paid for this with his life; Perceval, a rustic Welsh boy who became one of the most chivalrous knights at Camelot; Gawain, one of the bravest and most renowned knights in all of Britain, who accepted the terrifying Green Knight's challenge of the beheading game; Gawain's brothers, the sons of Morgause and King Lot of the Orkneys, Mordred (now accepted by Arthur), Agravaine, Gaheris and Gareth, the last of whom arrived in disguise at Camelot but won fame by defeating the Black, Green, Blue and Red knights to rescue the lady Lyonesse.

In the early days of the Round Table, Arthur's greatest knight was Gawain. He was a ferocious knight who lived for adventure but was eventually overshadowed by a knight from the overseas land of Benwick, whose name was Lancelot. Trained as a warrior by the Lady of the Lake, he was the greatest swordsman at the Round Table and he became Arthur's champion. Lancelot's son Galahad was the only knight able to sit at the Siege Perilous, a seat traditionally unoccupied at the Round Table. Merlin had once foretold that only the world's greatest and most chaste knight could sit there.

Sir Pelleas by Howard Pyle. Malory named Pelleas as one of only six knights who could better Gawain in combat.

One winter's night, as the Order sat awaiting their feast, a sound of thunder echoed around the hall of Camelot so loudly that it seemed as if the walls might collapse. The great hall went very dark, the thunder stopped and the hall was filled with a blinding light. As the knights shielded their eyes, a shimmering vision appeared over the centre of the Round Table. A white cloth suspended itself in the air, and underneath it was the shape of a great vessel; everyone who observed it sensed that it was a golden cup. As this hung in the air, a bountiful feast magically appeared on the Round Table. The veiled cup began to float up and away, carried out of the hall by an invisible force. And then it disappeared.

Arthur and his knights sat motionless. Galahad announced to the stunned audience that this was a vision of the Holy Grail, the most precious object in the Christian world. Arthur remembered a prophecy

of Merlin that the Holy Grail could protect Britain if presented to the High King, and he became obsessed with finding it. He summoned his 150 Knights of the Round Table, and sent them out to discover the Grail and return it to him to use for the good of all Britain.

Every knight of Arthur's court set out on his own personal Grail Quest. Many knights never returned, dying while attempting to fulfil their High King's order. As the knights quested, they ignored their other duties and Britain fell into decline, with barbarians raiding once more and pestilence spreading across the land.

Gawain quested long and hard, undertaking many adventures across the war-torn realm, but had no success. Upon his return to Camelot, he found that others had also given up in despair, many telling stories of the deaths of their fellow knights from all manner of mysterious beasts, evil knights, and unnatural pestilence. Arthur had never witnessed his knights suffer such defeat and disgrace, but remained meekly perched on his throne unable to think of anything but the Grail.

Arthur's other great knight, Lancelot, also failed. He entered the Grail Castle, the final resting place of the holy chalice, but as he attempted to lift the cloth covering the Grail, he felt a great pain surge through him and fell in agony. Healed by the Fisher King, the guardian of the Grail, Lancelot was told that he would never be able to take the chalice, as he was not pure and chaste enough to do so. Only a man without guilt would be able to lift the Grail. Upon his recovery Lancelot returned to Camelot.

Galahad quested through a desert, sensing that he was close to the end of his search. He met Perceval and Bors, both of whom had undertaken many brave adventures before arriving in the desert. The three knights rode together, and eventually they saw the same tall, dark castle that Lancelot had entered before them. The Fisher King greeted them courteously and explained that he was only permitted to allow the purest and most chivalrous man in the world to touch the Grail. Perceval did not address the Fisher King in the correct

Mural by Edwin Austin Abbey depicting Galahad and his knights receiving a blessing, in preparation for their search for the Holy Grail. (Library of Congress)

25

Mural by Edwin Austin Abbey depicting King Arthur standing at his throne as Joseph of Arimathea leads Galahad to the Seat Perilous at the Round Table. (Library of Congress)

courtly fashion, and so failed; Bors also failed to prove himself pure by refusing to repent his sins; Galahad stepped forward and the Fisher King realized that before him stood the purest knight in the world. He led the three knights into the hall of the Grail Castle, explaining that his work was complete and that Galahad would succeed him, and then he faded away. As Perceval and Bors looked on, Galahad strode towards the enshrouded chalice, and removed the cloth. He lifted the Grail, and the room was swathed in brilliant light. The rolling sound of thunder that had been present when the Grail first appeared at Camelot sounded once more, and both Galahad and chalice rose into the air and disappeared. The purest knight in the world had become the Grail's new guardian, and both had been magically moved to a secret new location. Neither the Grail nor Galahad was seen again during Arthur's reign.

Profoundly affected by the event he had witnessed, Perceval immediately became a monk, dying shortly afterwards, happy and fulfilled at having seen the Grail, but heartbroken that he had failed his king when the Grail was so close. Bors was able to return to Camelot to tell the High King what had happened.

The Grail had been found, but the Order of the Round Table had failed to bring it to Arthur. Merlin's prophecy therefore foretold doom. Certainly, while the knights were away on their quest, Britain had dissolved into chaos. Few good knights remained alive after the Grail Quest, and Arthur faced a struggle to regain stability in his kingdom.

Lancelot, returning from the Grail Quest, knew why he had been prevented from lifting the Grail. For several years, he had been in an adulterous affair with Guinevere. She had initially resisted Lancelot's charms, remaining devoted to Arthur, but eventually they began a passionate yet treasonous secret relationship. Mordred, Arthur's nephew, who had developed for himself a taste for mischief, was the only person to notice this.

Lancelot's return saw the resumption of the affair, and Mordred revealed this to Arthur. In a fury Arthur called for Guinevere to be tied to a stake and burned and for Lancelot to be banished from Camelot for evermore. Mordred dragged the queen to the stake and was in the process of setting a fire beneath it when Lancelot, along with his close friends Lionel and Bors, rushed into Camelot to save her. Some knights supported their king, while others, unable to stand by and watch their beloved queen murdered, sided with Lancelot. Lancelot's supporters managed to snatch the queen from the flames, and rushed her to Lancelot's stronghold of the Castle of the Joyous Gard, and then on to the continent to his homeland of Benwick.

Arthur declared war on Lancelot. Mordred urged Arthur to pursue Lancelot into Benwick and incite a battle; other knights urged caution. Yet Arthur's mind was made up when Mordred promised to act as his regent, ruling Britain for Arthur during the king's continental campaign. The High King, grateful to Mordred for revealing the queen's treason, agreed to Mordred's suggestion

The Holy Grail by Theodor Pixis. From Guerber's *Myths and Legends of the Middle Ages.* (Author's Collection)

Last Sleep of Arthur in Avalon
by Edward Burne-Jones.

and marched to war. The Order of the Round Table was broken and Britain fell further into the decline prophesised by Merlin.

Arthur crossed to the continent and marched to Benwick. Former comrades at the Round Table fought against each other; Gawain, wishing to avenge the death of his brothers at Lancelot's hand in the fight for Guinevere, fought bravely, but Lancelot held the queen safe.

News came from Camelot. Mordred had taken the throne for himself, and had invited the barbarian Saxons, Picts, and Irish to support him. Despite his fury towards Lancelot and Guinevere, Arthur chose to return to Britain to reclaim his realm.

Mordred took an axe to the Round Table, making it oblong with a prominent seat for himself at its head. Barbarian chieftains sat with him, feasting from Arthur's plentiful cellars. When Mordred heard of Arthur's imminent return, he mustered his horde of warriors and marched from Camelot to Dover, where he opposed Arthur's landing.

First from Arthur's ship was Gawain, his role as Arthur's champion restored after Lancelot's betrayal. He hacked down scores of Mordred's army, and the usurper's army retreated from him. As Mordred's army faded away, Gawain clashed with a huge enemy warrior and was killed at the very same moment as he slew his foe.

Arthur's army followed Mordred's retreating barbarians, and at Camlann on Salisbury Plain, the two armies drew up once again. Both sides were cautious – the Battle of Dover had been a bloodthirsty affair – and Arthur agreed to meet Mordred's chieftains in a parley. Kay advised against the meeting as he knew how treacherous Mordred could be, but Arthur hoped that Mordred would surrender without a fight.

Arthur and his finest knights rode to meet Mordred and his barbarian chieftains midway between the armies. Mordred wished only to mock Arthur, rather than appeal for peace. As they faced each other, one of Mordred's men drew his sword: An adder had bitten his ankle and he killed it without thinking. As he swung his weapon, Arthur's knights thought that this warrior was an assassin and struck him down. The battle began. The sky darkened and a storm broke. Ravens circled overhead, waiting to pick the flesh of the dead. The calamitous Battle of Camlann had begun.

Never had such a bloody battle been fought on British soil. Arthur's army was smaller than Mordred's, but the fight swung one way and then the other. Rain poured down and the battle lasted for hours. Eventually the rain tailed off, and Arthur surveyed the scene around him. He stood alone on a pile of bodies, and close by sat the loyal Bedivere, exhausted by the battle. Across the field of dead the High King spotted his usurper, and summoning all of his remaining energy, Arthur charged at Mordred and impaled him on a spear. Mordred, with the last of his strength, forced himself along the spear's shaft

Bedivere returns Excalibur to the lake as a miserable, mortally wounded Arthur looks on. From the *Roman de Saint Graal*, c. 1316. (British Library, London, UK / © British Library Board. All Rights Reserved / The Bridgeman Art Library)

and struck Arthur down with a blow to the head. Mordred fell dead, and in a faint of exhaustion and pain Arthur fell on top of him, mortally wounded.

Arthur was carried from the battlefield by the sole survivor, Bedivere. While he was doing so, the High King's pained voice spoke one final instruction to his loyal knight, telling him that Excalibur must be thrown into a lake. Bedivere, ever wanting to obey Arthur, agreed to do so, still hoping above all else that Arthur would recover from his wound. Knowing that Excalibur was a symbol of the High King's authority, he hid the sword rather than throwing it into the nearby lake. To discard Excalibur would be an act of treason.

Bedivere returned to Arthur and the High King weakly asked what had happened when the sword hit the water. Bedivere's answer was that the sword sunk below the surface; he had not been present when Arthur received Excalibur from the Lady of the Lake, and did not know of her existence. Arthur, angry despite his draining strength, told Bedivere to return and complete his instruction. Once more, Bedivere could not bring himself to do so, and returned with the same answer to Arthur's question. For a third

GAWAIN AND THE GREEN KNIGHT

Some aspects of Arthurian legend have their origin in pre-Christian symbolism. One such story is that of *Sir Gawain and the Green Knight*, which bears many similarities to the beheading stories found in Celtic myth. This plate shows Gawain arriving at the Green Chapel, keeping his appointment with the Green Knight.

᭡᭡•᭡᭡•᭡᭡•᭡᭡•᭡᭡•᭡᭡

On New Year's Day at Camelot, Gawain accepted the challenge of an otherworldly warrior, clad in green with green hair and green skin, carrying a pagan holly cluster. This Green Knight's challenge was that of a beheading game. The Green Knight dared any of Arthur's knights brave enough to deliver an undefended blow at the Green Knight's neck; if the Green Knight survived, the blow would be returned. Gawain stepped forward and beheaded the pagan champion with a mighty blow, but the Green Knight's torso stood up, picked up the head and commanded Gawain to arrive at the Green Chapel in a year's time to receive the return blow.

Gawain searched for the chapel for the full year and while staying with a knight named Bercilak, his host revealed the chapel's location. Bercilak's wife came to Gawain each night, kissing him and giving him a green baldric with magical powers of protection. Fearful of his coming meeting with the Green Knight, Gawain accepted this.

Arriving at the Green Chapel, the Green Knight twice made to deliver the blow, stopping short at Gawain's neck on both occasions and mocking Gawain for shaking with fear. He hafted the axe for a third time, and delivered the blow so skillfully that it did no more than nick Gawain's skin. Leaping to his feet, Gawain confronted the Green Knight, who turned out to be Sir Bercilak, bespelled by magic to test the honour of the Round Table. The first blow, Bercilak explained, was withheld as Gawain had honorably kept his appointment with certain death; the second he withheld as Gawain honorably spurned his wife's advances; yet the third was delivered, gently, for the dishonor of accepting the green baldric.

From that time on, Arthur decreed that Gawain's shield device would be a green baldric, so that all may know how he upheld the honor of the Round Table at the Green Chapel.

time, Arthur sent Bedivere to throw Excalibur to its watery grave, and this time, through his love for the king, Bedivere did so. As the blade neared the water, a feminine arm broke the lake's surface, gracefully caught the sword's hilt, flourished the blade three times, and slipped under the surface, taking Excalibur back into the watery realm of the Lady of the Lake.

Saddened by the symbolic end of Arthur's reign, Bedivere returned to his king and told him what he had seen. Now satisfied, Arthur asked Bedivere if he could be carried to the shoreline. Taking his king in his arms, Bedivere placed Arthur as he had wished, and watched as a black barge glided effortlessly across the water's surface to claim Arthur's wounded body.

The sun began to set and the black barge disappeared to the west. A mist swirled around, and the barge faded into it. When long gone, Bedivere heard Arthur's voice for one last time, whispering to him that nobody should mourn him, for he was departing to the enchanted Isle of Avalon, where his wounds would be magically healed by the Lady of the Lake. He would then be ready to return when Britain was in grave danger and the Britons needed him more than ever. From that day to this, Arthur has not returned.

Guinevere saw her days out as a nun, mourning the sins she had committed and her role in the fall of Arthur's great and happy kingdom. Lancelot returned to his tower, the Castle of the Joyous Gard in northern Britain, and lived in solitude, ashamed that his actions had led to Arthur's downfall. Bedivere, Arthur's last remaining loyal follower, died of old age, as did Lancelot, and with them ended the tale of Arthur's rule. The once and future king sleeps, awaiting his final summons by the British people. One day he shall return.

CHANGING NAMES AND PLACES

Some Arthurian characters familiar from Malory's work can be traced back as associates of Arthur from Celtic sources:

Bedivere: Bedwyr

Gawain: Gwalchmai

Guinevere: Gwenhwyfar

Kay: Cai

Mordred: Medraut (and a number of variant spellings), who is not always portrayed as Arthur's enemy

Although Arthur's main companions have remained constant over time, his court – named by Chrétien de Troyes as Camelot – has been located in many different places by writers and historians, including:

Cadbury Castle, Somerset

Caerleon, Gwent

Caerwent, Monmouthshire

Camelon, Stirlingshire

Chester, Cheshire

Colchester, Essex

Killibury, Cornwall

Montgomery, Powys

Winchester, Hampshire

Wroxeter, Shropshire

THE CELTIC ARTHUR

Wales, Cornwall, and the wider Celtic world are famous for their rich tradition of oral history. Not only did the medieval Celts attempt to record their past history – perhaps better considered as pseudo-history given the nature of some of the "facts"– but they also boasted one of the world's greatest collections of folklore and legend. Arthur featured in a number of these Celtic tales, some of which may contain a kernel of historical truth and some of which sit firmly within the realm of folklore.

The tales in this chapter were probably known a long time before they were written down, possibly being oral lore from earlier centuries. If this is the case, Arthur's legend could be far more ancient than we will ever be able to prove. Most early Arthurian sources have survived in their current form from twelfth- and thirteenth-century manuscripts, a time by which Arthur's fame was widespread beyond the Celtic lands.

As a footnote to this chapter it should be remembered that when these tales were first recited, the difference between the Arthur of history and the Arthur of legend was blurred at best: a distinction between the two rarely mattered in the Celtic stories.

Arthur did not always appear in the guise of a heroic warrior or king; some of the stories make him appear foolish, rash, or spiteful. The Arthur of the Celts was a very different man from the chivalric, righteous ruler of medieval English and French stories.

Histories and Annals

Preserved in a book dating to the twelfth century is a collection of Welsh writing with a far earlier origin. One of these texts is crucial to the shaping of Arthurian history and legend: *The Welsh Annals* (*Annales Cambriae*). Annals were mostly used to record the births and deaths of saints and kings, and significant

Sir Mordred by H. J. Ford. Mordred was connected to Arthur from an early date: *The Welsh Annals* named him as Medraut and recorded that both he and Arthur fought at the Battle of Camlann. (Author's Collection)

historic events; in broad terms, *The Welsh Annals* reads as a timeline of history, and two entries refer to Arthur:

> 518 CE The Battle of Badon, in which Arthur carried the cross of our lord Jesus Christ for three days and three nights on his shoulders, and the Britons were the victors.
> 539 CE The conflict at Camlann in which Arthur and Medraut perished; and there was pestilence in Britain and Ireland.

The exact years recorded in the *Annals* are disputed, with some historians placing events up to 25 years earlier (Badon taking place in the 490s and Camlann in the 510s). If the entries are accurate accounts of true-life events, these years pinpoint the life of a very real Arthur as a post-Roman British leader. Unfortunately, there is no corroborating evidence that can prove for certain that these events were genuine, or, even if they were, whether Arthur's name was an original feature or inserted at a later date. It is also possible that without any earlier sources to rely on, the *Annals'* writer may have taken an educated guess at the real Arthur's dates, based on surviving oral tradition. Another alternative is that *Annals'* dates were artificially constructed to demonstrate that Arthur really did live, rather than condemning him as a dateless legend. Such options are commonplace and plentiful for many Celtic Arthurian sources.

The question of Medraut's role is an interesting one. *The Welsh Annals* do not state that he fought against Arthur, yet this became an essential ingredient of later Arthurian legend as Arthur's final battle against Mordred. Some Cornish tales actually favour him as a hero, and the Cornish spelling of his name was popular for some time. Perhaps this hints at Medraut as a Cornish leader, who may have fought against a non-Cornish Arthur.

The reference to the Battle of Badon is equally significant as it is referred to in a different British source written in the sixth century: Gildas's *The Ruin of Britain* (*De Excidio Britanniae*) tells us that the Britons were led by Ambrosius Aurelianus, who fought off Saxon invaders some time around 500.

> With him our people regained their strength, challenged the enemy to battle, and, the Lord acceding, victory fell to us. From then on our citizens and then the enemies conquered… This lasted up until the year of the siege of Badon Hill, almost the most recent defeat of the Saxons and certainly not the least. That was the year of my birth, and as I know since then forty-four years and one month have already passed.

Sadly, Gildas does not mention Arthur's name anywhere in his writings. Some later tales suggested that Arthur killed Gildas's brother, and Gildas then discarded all references to Arthur's great deeds from his text.

Surviving in the same manuscript that holds *The Welsh Annals* is *The History of the Britons* (*Historia Brittonum*). The author identifies himself as Nennius, a ninth-century British monk; the actual author has been disputed but the manuscript can be dated to around 829 or 830. The earliest surviving copy we have today was written around 1100.

The narrative contains fictional, magical elements, but some half-remembered history might also be present. *The History* claims that a British leader named Vortigern was betrayed by his Saxon ally Hengist, and this broadly tallies with Gildas's account of the period. With Hengist's revolt, Saxon kingdoms in Britain expanded, but were held back by the victories of a war leader named Arthur who fought for the British kings. *The History* does not name Arthur as a king, actually implying that he was not, and instead describes him as a "leader of battles" (*dux bellorum*). A list of Arthur's victories is given: none can be identified with any certainty – or even if they were real battles – although we may assume from the context of the passage that his enemies were probably Saxons. *The History* does not say what became of Arthur, nor does it mention his other famous battle, that at Camlann, where tradition (and *The Welsh Annals*) remembered that he was killed.

A reconstruction of the fortress of Tintagel in the post-Roman period. Artwork by Peter Dennis. (Osprey Publishing)

With the death of Hengist, Octha his son came from the northern part of Britain to the kingdom of Kent. At that time, Arthur fought against them with the kings of the Britons, for he was the leader of battles. The first battle was in the east at the river that is called Glein. The second, third, fourth and fifth battles were by another river called Dubglas in the region of Linnuis. The sixth battle was by the river that is named Bassas. The seventh battle was in the wood of Caledonia, that is Cat Coed Celyddon. The eighth battle was in the fort of Guinnion, in which Arthur carried the image of the Virgin Mary upon his shoulders and the pagans were turned around in a rout, and there was a great slaughter of them through the might of our Lord Jesus Christ and through the might of the Virgin Mary. The ninth battle was fought in the City of the Legion. He fought the tenth battle on the bank of the river which is called Tribruit. The eleventh battle was made on the mount that is called Agned. The twelfth battle was on Mount Badon, in which nine hundred and sixty men fell from one charge of Arthur's; and no-one laid them low except he; and he showed himself victor in all his battles.

Later in the manuscript Arthur is featured again in a collection of local folklore.

There is another wonder in the region called Buellt. There is a mass of stones and one stone is placed on the top of the pile with the footprint of a dog on it. When Cafall, the dog of the soldier Arthur, hunted the boar Troynt, he pressed his footprint into a stone, after which Arthur gathered a pile of stones underneath it and it was called Carn Cafall. Men come and carry the stones in their hands for a distance of a day and a night and on the next day the stone is found back on the pile.

There is another wonder in the region called Erging. A grave is next to a spring, which is called Llygad Amr, and the name of the man buried there is Amr son of Arthur the soldier, who killed him and buried him there. And men come to measure the tomb and it is sometimes six feet long, sometimes nine feet long, sometimes twelve feet long, and sometimes fifteen feet long. At whatever length you measure it at one time, you will not find it again at the same length. I have tested this myself.

The reference to Arthur as a "soldier" reinforces the idea that he was not himself a king; at the same time, the movement of the stones and the variable grave length demonstrate Arthur's place in folklore even at this early date. The mention of the hunt for the boar connects with *Culhwch and Olwen* (a Celtic Arthurian tale detailed in the next section), and the reference to Arthur killing his own son is one of several different versions of the death of Arthur's shadowy child.

In one late twelfth- or early thirteenth-century manuscript of *The History of the Britons* is an addition that may represent later tales associated with

Arthur, or another otherwise forgotten Arthurian tradition. This manuscript, the annotations within it being known as *The Sawley Glosses,* was written in Yorkshire and suggests that this was an attempt to link the king of popular medieval tales to Wedale in this region.

'Son of Uthr' that is 'son of the horrible' since he was cruel from childhood. 'Arthur' translated into Latin means 'horrible bear' or 'iron hammer' with which the jaws of lions were broken.

Then Arthur went to Jerusalem, and there he made a cross in the same size as the Blessed Cross. And there it was consecrated. And for three continuous days he fasted and kept vigil and prayed in the presence of the Holy Cross, so that the Lord granted to him a victory over the pagans, and that was done. And then he himself carried the image of Holy Mary, the pieces of which were thus saved in great veneration at Wedale.

THE BOAR KING IS CORNERED (NEXT PAGE)

Welsh tradition recorded a campaign by Arthur against the enchanted boar king Twrch Trwyth or Troynt and his piglets. The boars were originally a sinful king and his sons who were magically transformed by a curse to ravage Ireland. In *Culhwch and Olwen*, Arthur's men were tasked with collecting a razor, comb, and shears lodged in between the boar king's ears. In the fighting, Arthur's son Llachau is slain by the boars. It has been suggested that this tale remembers a campaign between an historical Arthur and Irish raiders in south Wales: much of the action can be traced on a route through Gwent and Dyfed, and the boars originally arrive from Ireland.

This plate shows one of several bloody battles between Arthur's men and the boars; the hunt was a deadly running battle fought across Ireland, Wales, and the south-western British peninsula. Gwyn Jones and Thomas Jones' *The Mabinogion* (published in 1949) described one of the battles:

Arthur summoned to him Gwyn son of Nudd and asked him whether he knew aught of Twrch Trwyth. He said he did not. Thereupon all the huntsmen went to hunt the pigs as far as Dyffryn Llychwr. And Grugyn Silver-bristle and Llwydawg the Hewer dashed into them and slew the huntsmen so that not a soul of them escaped alive, save one man only. So Arthur and his hosts came to the place where Grugyn and Llwydawg were. And then he let loose upon them all the dogs that had been named to this end. And at the clamour that was then raised, and the barking, Twrch Trwyth came up and defended them. And ever since they had crossed the Irish Sea, he had not set eyes on them till now. Then was he beset by men and dogs. With might and with main he went to Mynydd Amanw, and then a pigling was slain of his pigs. And then they joined with him life for life, and it was then Twrch Llawin was slain. And then another of his pigs was slain, Gwys was his name. And he then went to Dyffryn Amanw, and there Banw and Benwig were slain. Not one of his pigs went with him alive from that place, save Grugyn Silver-bristle and Llwydawg the Hewer.

Culhwch and Olwen

Culhwch and Olwen (*Culhwch ac Olwen*) survives today in two different manuscripts: one dated to approximately 1350, and the other dated between 1385 and 1410. It is one of the most complete and lengthy early Celtic stories of Arthur, and may be an attempt to pull together many strands of the legend into one cohesive tale, or a way of dropping Arthur into other folk tales not previously featuring him.

Culhwch and Olwen reads very much like a fairytale, and is included as one of the 11 stories in the nineteenth-century collection *The Mabinogion*.

⟡•⟡•⟡•⟡•⟡•⟡

Culhwch arrived at the court of his cousin Arthur – chief lord of the Island of Britain – on a swift horse accompanied by his two spotted greyhounds. A toothless hag had foretold that he would marry Olwen, the beautiful daughter of the giant Ysbaddaden, and he now came to Arthur to help him to fulfil this prophecy.

Culhwch arrived mid-feast, and although Cai tried to send him away, the ever generous Arthur instead offered Culhwch any gift he wished for, other than Arthur's most prized possessions: his ship and his mantle, his sword Caledfwlch, his spear Rhongomyniad, his shield Wynebgwrthucher, his dagger Carnwennan, and his wife Gwenhwyfar.

Culhwch's request was simple: he asked for Arthur's assistance in marrying Olwen.

For a full year, Arthur's messengers searched for Ysbaddaden and Olwen, but none found them. So Arthur despatched six of his greatest warriors to help Culhwch: Cai, who could breathe underwater for nine nights, go without sleep for nine nights, and inflict wounds that would not heal; Bedwyr, a handsome warrior who could draw blood from his enemies faster than anyone; Cynddylig Gyfarwydd, the best scout in Arthur's court; Gwrhwr Gwalstawd, who spoke all languages of man and beast; Gwalchmai – Arthur's nephew – a great horseman; and Menw, who could cast spells to keep them safe. These six set out with Culhwch to find Ysbaddaden's fortress.

Eventually coming upon it, they slew the nine gatekeepers and their nine mastiff guard dogs. Ysbaddaden was so huge that his eyelids were held open with forks, such was their weight; and Olwen was as beautiful as Culhwch had hoped. Culhwch asked for Olwen's hand in marriage, but Ysbaddaden drove them away three times, each time trying to kill Culhwch with a stone spear. Wounded each time by Arthur's warriors, Ysbaddaden then set 40 near-impossible tasks for Culhwch: if all were completed, Ysbaddaden would allow Olwen to marry him.

The seven warriors set about their tasks. The first was to bring Ysbaddaden the sword of Wrnach the giant; Cai tricked Wrnach into thinking he was a

swordsmith and Cai killed him with the giant's own sword. Taking this sword for Ysbaddaden, the seven were joined by Arthur and more of his warriors. Arthur aided with the next challenge, helping to free Eidoel prisoner of Gliwi.

Gwrhwr Gwalstawd then helped with the next quest: locating Mabon son of Modron. Gwrhwr Gwalstawd talked to a blackbird, a stag, an owl, an eagle, and finally a salmon, who explained that Mabon would be found imprisoned further up the river. Cai and Gwrhwr Gwalstawd travelled upstream on the salmon's back to help Arthur's besieging warriors successfully to rescue Mabon.

Next, Arthur's warriors sailed in his ship *Prydwen* to hunt the shape-shifting she-wolf Rhymhi and her whelps. After that success, Gwrhwr Gwalstawd saved an anthill from a fire and the ants brought to him the special flax seed that Ysbaddaden had set as the next test. Cai and Bedwyr then trapped Dillus the Bearded while he slept and cut off his beard, which was to be presented to Ysbaddaden to show that challenge's completion.

Arthur sang a song mocking Cai's cowardly behaviour towards Dillus and Cai stormed off, never to help Arthur again. Even without Cai, Arthur and his men won other victories and completed more of Ysbaddaden's tasks. They fought men and enchanted animals, and took the tusks from the mighty tusked boar Ysgithrwyn Pen Baedd.

Arthur's warriors next set out to Ireland to take the Cauldron of Diwrnach, the steward of the king of Ireland. After a feast in Ireland, Bedwyr stole the cauldron and Arthur's servant Hygwydd carried it away while the rest of Arthur's warriors killed the Irish warriors who opposed them. Fighting off the rest of the warriors of Ireland on the way back to the coast, Arthur's warband boarded *Prydwen* with the cauldron overflowing with Irish treasure. Another task was completed.

An Italian mosaic pavement depicting King Arthur, c. 1166. (Otranto Cathedral, Italy / Alinari / The Bridgeman Art Library)

Next was the hunting of the poisonous boar king Twrch Trwyth – the Hog Chief – and his seven piglets. Twrch Trwyth had recently destroyed a third of Ireland, and Menw turned himself into a bird to find the boar king and tried to snatch a razor, shears, and comb held on the boar's deadly bristles; Ysbaddaden had demanded these be delivered to him so that he could trim his hair and beard with them. Menw was caught by Twrch Trwyth and crippled by the boar's poisonous spines. Returning to Ireland, Arthur and his huntsmen pursued Twrch Trwyth with dogs for nine days and nine nights. In this time only one of the piglets was killed. Gwrhwr Gwalstawd turned himself into a bird and tried to talk to the boar king, without success. Twrch Trwyth and his remaining piglets swam to Wales and laid waste to the south, pursued by Arthur all the time. Eventually brought to bay, Twrch Trwyth killed many of Arthur's warriors and Arthur's warriors killed the piglets, but the boar king escaped into the River Severn and then to Cornwall. Twrch Trwyth finally fled into the sea, never to be seen again: but Arthur had succeeded in taking his razor, shears, and comb.

Collecting blood from the Very Black Witch was the last task. She lived in a cave in the uplands of hell and defeated four of Arthur's warriors before he himself went to the cave and split her in two with his knife Carnwennan. Caw of Prydyn collected the blood and this final task was completed.

Returning to Ysbaddaden, Culhwch took Olwen as his wife, and Ysbaddaden was dragged to a mound and beheaded. And that is how Culhwch won Olwen, daughter of Ysbaddaden.

The Spoils of the Otherworld

The Spoils of the Otherworld (*Preideu Annwfyn*) is a poem attributed to the great northern British bard Taliesin. If this is accurate, this means it was composed in the sixth century and would therefore be a very early story about Arthur.

The Spoils of the Otherworld is a curious piece in that it shows Arthur being defeated in battle. Other early tales sometimes show him being outsmarted or ridiculed by saints, but seldom do we hear of Arthur's band of warriors being so utterly vanquished in early literature.

It also places him in a supernatural environment, showing that Arthur's name was detached from purely historical deeds at an early date. The story at the centre of *The Spoils of the Otherworld* is probably even older than the sixth century, perhaps predating the Roman invasion of Britain. It mirrors a type of adventure remembered in much older Celtic myth, in *Culhwch and Olwen*, and in medieval romance as the Grail Quest … a quest for a cauldron.

Lancelot and the Dwarf by H. J. Ford. Dwarves usually appear in medieval Arthurian legend as cunning servants and squires to knights. (Author's Collection)

LANCELOT & THE DWARF.

❧•❧•❧•❧•❧•❧

Gwair – one of the three exalted prisoners of Britain – was held in heavy grey chains in a faerie fortress in Annwn, the Otherworld realm of magic and the dead. But Arthur, in his ship *Prydwen*, along with three boatloads of warriors, sailed both to free him and to take for themselves the Cauldron of Annwn.

This mighty cauldron was blue about its edge with pearl, and was never able to boil a coward's food; it belonged to the Lord of Annwn and was warmed by the breath of nine witches.

Arthur and his warriors disembarked from their ships and attacked the Otherworld's fortresses: the Fort of Four Corners, the Fort of Intoxication, the Fort of Ice, the Fort of Glass, and the Fort of Destruction. The battle-hardened warriors then pressed on to assault the Divine Fort, and finally the Mound Fort.

A battle followed at the gates of hell, and from Arthur's army the sword of lightning slaughter flashed against the three-score hundred Otherworld warriors who fought against him.

Three boatloads in Arthur's *Prydwen* went to sea, but except for seven men, none of those warriors returned from this woeful conflict.

The Dream of Rhonabwy

The Dream of Rhonabwy (*Breuddwyd Rhonabwy*) was probably composed between 1149 and 1159. The fictional character Rhonabwy set out on a mission for Madog ap Maredudd, who was the ruler of Powys at this time. Regardless of the tale's original date, *The Dream of Rhonabwy* is a very curious piece.

The story appears to show an inverted world: Arthur is a weak and distracted leader, the Battle of Camlann occurs before Badon, and Arthur is bettered by a lesser warlord named Owain. Owain's inclusion in the piece is interesting, as he was a late sixth century northern British leader, otherwise unconnected to the Welsh borders but eventually to become the knight Yvain in medieval literature.

⁊•⁊•⁊•⁊•⁊•⁊

The Coming of Guinevere by Aubrey Beardsley. In Celtic tales, Guinevere was named Gwenhwyfar. (Author's Collection)

Madog ap Maredudd was at war. Of the warriors serving Madog, Rhonabwy was one; while on campaign for his lord he settled to sleep in an unkempt hovel. He dreamed.

Rhonabwy and his warband were at the River Severn, and were greeted by Iddog ap Mynio; at the Battle of Camlann seven years previously, Iddog had caused the battle with his poisonous tongue but now served as a messenger of Arthur the Emperor. Rhonabwy travelled with Iddog to the ford at Rhyd-y-Groes where Arthur had mustered a military camp. Arthur's army were preparing to fight against the Saxon chieftain Osla Big Knife at the Battle of Badon, and Rhonabwy saw Arthur consulting with his advisors Gwarthegyd ap Caw and Bishop Bedwini.

Arthur's army assembled, with warriors coming from far and wide, and he was presented with his sword: a glorious blade with two serpents on its golden hilt. Seated on his throne atop a white cloak as his army prepared for war, Arthur played the chess-like board game gwyddbwyll with Owain ap Urien.

As they played, messengers arrived. The first messenger informed Owain that Arthur's warriors were teasing Owain's ravens. Owain asked Arthur to call them off, but was ignored. The second messenger informed Owain that

Arthur's warriors were now killing Owain's ravens. Owain asked Arthur to call them off, but was ignored. The third messenger informed Owain that the most noble of his ravens were now dead. Owain complained to Arthur but was told to play on.

Mid-game, Owain instructed Gwres of Rheged to raise the warband's battle flag, and his ravens then fought back against Arthur's warriors with a steely resolve. A fourth messenger arrived at the game and informed Arthur that Owain's ravens were now slaying his warriors. Arthur asked Owain to call them off, but was told to play on. A fifth messenger arrived to tell Arthur once more that his warriors were being killed, and again Arthur was told to play on.

At the arrival of a sixth messenger, who informed Arthur that the ravens had slaughtered the most noble of his warriors, the emperor rose from the game and crushed the pieces to dust. Owain called his ravens off, and Osla Big Knife arrived to beg for peace.

… Rhonabwy awoke.

Tales of the Bards

Arthur appears as a character in many other Welsh literary pieces. Some are no more than passing references, or links to characters or events seen elsewhere in Arthurian legend. But some are complete or fragmentary stories relating to Arthur himself, the most intriguing excerpts from which are gathered in this section.

THE RAID FOR THE CAULDRON (NEXT PAGE)

A recurring theme in Arthurian legend is the raid for a cauldron. In Celtic tales, this plot device is the central theme of the poem *The Spoils of the Otherworld* (*Preideu Annwfyn*) and also appears as a task in *Culhwch and Olwen,* where Arthur and his warriors steal the Cauldron of Diwrnach in Ireland.

Similarities between both stories suggest that they might share a provenance: this may originally have been the same story told in the Second Branch of the *Mabinogi* about a quest for a cauldron in Ireland by the hero giant Bran. In medieval stories of Arthur, the Knights of the Round Table search for the Holy Grail, which is just possibly a Christian reinvention of the earlier tales.

This plate shows Arthur's warriors attempting to steal the Cauldron of Annwn from the faerie Otherworld. Arthur's men fend off the warriors of the Otherworld, while attempting to drag away the magical cauldron.

The poem states that only seven warriors returned in defeat after besieging several faerie fortresses searching for both the cauldron and a prisoner named Gwair.

In Celtic mythology the Otherworld is usually shown as a paradise with abundant feasting and eternal youth, but both Irish and Welsh tales also show a darker underworld within: in Irish tales this is ruled by Donn the god of the dead, and his Welsh counterpart is most likely the Lord of Annwn.

The cauldron itself is described better than any other aspect of the story:

From the breath of nine witches it was heated.
The Lord of Annwn's cauldron, how did it look?
Dark blue around the edge with pearl,
It boils not the food of a coward, it has not been so destined.

The Stanzas of the Graves (*Englynion y Beddau*) is a work of verse that is difficult to date precisely. It recalled the sites of graves of heroic figures from the past, and along with references to Gwalchmai, Owain son of Urien, and the Battle of Camlann, *The Stanzas* note that a grave for Arthur is "the world's wonder," meaning that its location is no longer remembered. This may be an early reference to the claim that Arthur would return as a saviour of the nation, until which time he slept in a magical cave or island. The Arthur stanza reads:

> A grave for March, a grave for Gwythur.
> A grave for Gwgon Red-Sword.
> The world's wonder a grave for Arthur.

Appearing in the same manuscript as *The Stanzas of the Graves* is the otherwise untitled piece *Pa Gur*. This title is from the opening line of the poem, which translates as: "What man is the gatekeeper?" Usually dated to the eleventh century, *Pa Gur* survives as an incomplete work, but some elements of the story reflect events included in *Culhwch and Olwen*. What we do know is that the piece recites a conversation between Arthur and Glewlwyd the gatekeeper, and it later develops into a list of the deeds of Arthur and his men, defending Britons up and down the island from monstrous creatures of folklore. Excerpts showing Arthur and his followers fighting against these supernatural enemies include:

> Although Arthur was playing,
> her blood flowed
> in the hall of Afarnach,
> fighting, Arthur and the witch.
> He pierced the club-headed warrior
> in the dwellings of Disethach.
> At the mountain of Edinburgh
> he fought against dog-headed warriors.
>
> On the shores of Tryfrwyd
> Fighting against the grey wolfman
> Bedwyr was ferocious
> With sword and shield.
>
> At the peak of Ystanfngwn
> Cai slew nine witches
> Cai the Fair went to Anglesey
> to hunt lions
> His shield was polished
> against the cat of Palug.
> When people ask

'Who killed the cat of Palug?'
Nine-score warriors
would fall as its food;
Nine-score champions.

The Dialogue of Arthur and the Eagle (*Ymddiddan Arthur a'r Eryr*) survives in a fourteenth century manuscript, although it is probably of earlier origin. It consists of a conversation between Arthur, who describes himself as a bard, and a great bird revealed to be Eliwlod, grandson of Uther and nephew of Arthur; Eliwlod has been magically transformed into bird form. The meeting takes place in Cornwall, and Arthur is referred to as "Chief of the Battalions of Cornwall" rather than as a king, and also as a "bear of men." Of the observations by the eagle about Arthur, we are told:

Arthur and Guinevere by H. J. Ford. (Author's Collection)

> Arthur who has achieved far-flung fame,
> bear of men, joyous host,
> the eagle has seen you before.

> Arthur of the terrifying sword,
> your enemies will not stand before your charge.
> I am the son of Madog son of Uthr.

> Arthur, undaunted in battle,
> path of the fallen,
> kinship to you is fitting.

The Dialogue of Gwenhwyfar and Arthur (*Ymddiddan Gwenhwyfar ac Arthur*) has survived in two manuscripts from the sixteenth and seventeenth centuries. These two versions have differences, but both consist of a conversation between two or three characters. Although the characters are not named, they appear to be Arthur's wife Gwenhwyfar, a warlord named Melwas, and possibly Cai; Arthur is mentioned only once by name, and despite the poem's title, he does not seem to be present in this conversation.

The atmosphere is one of friction between Melwas and Gwenhwyfar, possibly leading to her abduction by Melwas that features in other early Arthurian tradition; Cai's role is that of Gwenhwyfar's bodyguard. The tone of the poem is shown in the following stanzas:

Melwas:
Gwenhwyfar of the arrogant gaze,
Tell me if you remember
The place where you saw me before.

Gwenhwyfar:
I saw a plain man
At Arthur's long table in Devon
Sharing wine out to his company.

Melwas:
Gwenhwyfar of the foolish tongue,
Such stupid words come from the mouth of a woman,
There indeed you saw me.

The poem *I Have Been* (*Mi a Fûm*) does not feature Arthur, but does recall his son Llachau. Dated to the tenth or eleventh centuries, this poem is one of several early references to the death of Arthur's son, suggesting that this may originally have been an important story that gradually faded from prominence. Passing glimpses of Arthur's son are seen in *The History of the Britons* (where he is named Amr), *Pa Gur* (where he fights alongside Cai), and *Culhwch and Olwen*, where he is slain fighting against Twrch Trwyth.

I have been where Llachau was slain,
the son of Arthur, terrible at singing,
when ravens flew over the dead.

THE ARTHURIAN TRIADS

The triads were verses of Welsh folklore recited as stories in threes. The earliest triads surviving today were written down in the thirteenth to fifteenth centuries, but had almost certainly originated at earlier date. Some of these include Arthur as one of the three main characters of the triad, or as a fourth even more important character. This may indicate a later addition based on his medieval popularity or may suggest that Arthur had a long tradition of being a hero valued above all others, worthy of his own entries in the triads.

Three battle horsemen of Arthur's court
Three chieftains of Arthur's court
Three exalted prisoners of the Island of Britain
Three faithless wives of the Island of Britain
Three fortunate concealments of the Island of Britain
Three frivolous bards of the Island of Britain

Three futile battles of the Island of Britain
Three generous men of the Island of Britain
Three great queens of Arthur
Three harmful blows of the Island of Britain
Three mistresses of Arthur
Three peers of Arthur's court
Three powerful swineherds of the Island of Britain
Three red reapers of the Island of Britain
Three rich men of the Island of Britain
Three skilful bards at Arthur's court
Three splendid maidens of Arthur's court
Three tribal thrones of the Island of Britain
Three unfortunate disclosures
Three unrestrained ravagings of the Island of Britain
Three unrestricted guests of Arthur's court
Three who could not be expelled from Arthur's court

Lives of the Saints

The Lives of the Saints are not a single collection of hagiography, but describe a style of medieval Welsh ecclesiastical storytelling supposedly based on historical events. They were most probably recorded before Geoffrey of Monmouth's retelling of the Arthurian legend.

A real-life Arthur could not have lived across the time period of the lives of all of the saints he is linked to, but Arthur's role in the Lives of the Saints is significant regardless of historical authenticity. He is presented as a complex character with many more dimensions than his later medieval self. He appears in the Lives as a warrior and a leader of men, but does not always appear to be a king; perhaps the authors of the Lives expected their audience to know Arthur's status, or perhaps he was deliberately kept as a shadowy figure to avoid eclipsing the true heroes of the Lives, the saints themselves.

The stained glass windows at St Carantoc's Church in Crantock, Cornwall, illustrate the tale of Arthur and Carannog. The saint is traditionally accompanied by a dove. (S. Tyson)

In the Life of St Illtud, Arthur was Illtud's cousin. Illtud himself was a great warrior in his day, and decided to visit his cousin to observe the household of a champion so renowned as Arthur. Illtud set sail from Brittany, and was impressed with Arthur's host of warriors and the generosity of the king.

The Life of St Carannog told how the saint met Arthur at the Severn Estuary, which was ruled by Arthur; Arthur's warriors were intending to use Carannog's altar as a table, and Arthur told Carannog that the altar would be returned to him if he proved himself useful. Arthur was hunting a dragon that had laid waste to this part of his kingdom, so Carannog helped Arthur to find the dragon. When Carannog came face to face with the fiery beast, it meekly bowed its head before him. He then ordered the dragon to depart, causing no harm to Arthur's kingdom in the future. In return, Arthur returned the altar and granted Carannog new land, upon which the saint built a church and monastery.

The Life of St Euflamm saw Arthur once again in combat against a dragon, this time in Brittany where Arthur searched out fierce monsters to slay. Arthur, armed with a club and lion-skin shield, fought against the dragon for a whole day but could not deliver a blow deadly enough to slay the creature. In a break from fighting, Arthur went in search of water and was assisted by Euflamm, who prayed for water to be granted by God. Miraculously, water sprang from a rock and Arthur was refreshed; he also begged the saint to give him a blessing, which Euflamm did. In the end, Euflamm himself vanquished the dragon through the power of prayer, where Arthur's weapons had failed.

However, not all saintly Lives are so complimentary of Arthur, instead portraying him in a very different light.

In the Life of St Padarn, the saint was in his church when the tyrant Arthur came inside. Arthur liked the tunic that Padarn wore, given to Padarn in Jerusalem, and demanded it from him. Padarn refused, and Arthur stormed out in a blazing fury. Upon his return, Arthur demanded that the tunic be handed over to him. Padarn suggested that the earth should swallow up such a greedy man, and so it did, right up to Arthur's chin. Arthur apologized to God and Padarn, asking for forgiveness for his anger and greed. This was granted, and Arthur took Padarn as his patron, leaving as a better man than he arrived.

In the Life of St Cadog, Arthur intervened in a feud between two rival kings. King Brychan's daughter had been kidnapped by a warband of three hundred men belonging to his rival king named Gwynllyw. A battle ensued

ARTHUR IN BATTLE POEMS

The Gododdin (Y Gododdin) is a northern British poem remembering an army of British warriors who rode to their deaths in a battle that took place around 600 CE. The location of the battle is no longer known, but Catterick in North Yorkshire is commonly suggested.

Although the British warriors were almost completely wiped out, the poet tells us that they fought bravely, and commends many individual deeds. Among the glorious dead is Gwawrddur and we are told that:

> He glutted black ravens on the wall
> Of a fort, though he were no Arthur

So Gwawrddur killed many enemies, but he was not as great a warrior as Arthur. The written version of Y Gododdin survives in two late thirteenth-century manuscripts; the style of language in the Arthur stanza suggests that it was present in the tenth or eleventh centuries at the very latest. But if this reference is contemporary with the battle itself, Y Gododdin contains the oldest known reference to Arthur and acknowledges him as a warrior of renown even at this early date. It does not, unfortunately, tell us whether he was a real or legendary hero.

Geraint Son of Erbin (Geraint Filius Erbin) shows Arthur in the role of a warlord or emperor. Purporting to tell the tale of the Battle of Llongborth, Geraint dates at least as far back as the ninth century and is perhaps even older. This makes it another early addition to Arthurian literature, and demonstrates that Arthur was considered to be a worthy battle hero at that time. Geraint was a Dumnonian prince (in modern Devon and Cornwall) and the poem records the defeat of his army at Llongborth; alongside Geraint fought Arthur's "brave men." Geraint features in later Arthurian literature as the knight Erec, and is himself addressed as a great warrior in this poem. The Arthur stanza reads:

> At Llongborth I saw Arthur's
> brave men, they hewed with steel,
> emperor, leader in toil.

An alternative version reads:

> At Llongborth were slain Arthur's
> brave men, they hewed with steel,
> emperor, leader in toil.

on the border between the two kingdoms, and Gwynllyw's men were badly mauled, losing two hundred of their number. Gwynllyw escaped with Brychan's daughter still in his clutches, but came across Arthur, Cai, and Bedwyr sitting at the crest of a hill playing dice games. Arthur was tempted to kill Gwynllyw and rape the girl, but Cai and Bedwyr reminded him that it was their duty to aid those in distress. Arthur questioned Gwynllyw as to the nature of the feud, and then asked upon whose land they were standing. Gwynllyw announced to Arthur that they were in his kingdom, so Arthur, Cai, and Bedwyr lent their support to his cause, defeating Brychan and allowing Gwynllyw to steal his rival's daughter to marry: Cadog himself being their first born son.

Later in the tale of Cadog, a man arrived at Cadog's monastery seeking sanctuary, as he had killed three of Arthur's warriors. The fugitive stayed with Cadog for seven years, until Arthur eventually hunted him down, and told Cadog that sanctuary could not be given for such a lengthy period of time. In a parley, it was decided that Arthur was owed one hundred cows as compensation for his warriors' deaths; Arthur pedantically announced that the cows should be red at the front and white at the back, otherwise he would not accept them. Cadog managed to find one hundred such beasts with divine intervention, and handed them over to Arthur at a ford in a river. As Arthur's warriors waded in to round the cows up, the animals turned into bundles of fern and washed away. Arthur was forced to admit that he had been bettered by the saint, and agreed that sanctuary could be given for a further seven months and seven days.

The Lady of the Lake receiveth the sword Excalibur by Aubrey Beardsley. (Author's Collection)

The Life of St Gildas explained that he was a contemporary of Arthur, the king of the whole of Britain. Although Gildas was loyal to his king, the saint's 23 brothers fought against Arthur, refusing to accept him as their king. Huail, Gildas's eldest brother, frequently defeated the king in battle, but was on one occasion pursued to the Isle of Man where Arthur slew him. Upon hearing this news, Gildas forgave Arthur for the murder of Huail (although another tradition suggested that Gildas never forgave Arthur and wrote him out of history). Later in the tale Arthur's army besieged the city of Glastonbury. He did this as the rebellious King Melwas had raped Gwenhwyfar and taken her to Glastonbury as his hostage. Arthur commanded the entire armies of both Cornwall and Devon, and only when Gildas intervened was the situation diffused.

YE·ANCIENT·CITY·OF·CAMELOT·

Ye Ancient City of Camelot by Aubrey Beardsley. (Author's Collection)

Breton Tales

The Breton stories of Arthur bridge a literary gap between the Arthur of medieval French literature and the Arthur of the Celtic world. In the fifth and sixth centuries, Brittany became a continental power base for British warlords. With them came their social and cultural history and whether at this time or slightly later, Arthur came to feature in their local legends.

The idea that Arthur was a "once and future king" – that he would one day return when the Celtic people needed him the most – may have originated in Brittany. The original stories of Arthur's famous Round Table may also have developed here – the medieval writer Wace claimed to have first heard of the Round Table from Breton folk tales – and a number of twelfth-century songs recited some of the more fantastical stories about Arthur and his promised return from the dead.

Away from the realm of folklore, the *Legend of St Goeznovius* suggested that Arthur cleared swathes of Breton land from Saxon dominance in the fifth century, before chaos descended upon his death.

The Saxons, pagan demonic men striving to shed blood by their very nature, afflicted the Britons. Their pride was suppressed for a time by the great Arthur, king of the Britons, so that they were repelled for the most part and compelled to serve him. But when the same Arthur, after many victories which he famously won in Britain and parts of Gaul, was called forth from human affairs, the way was again open to the Saxons, by which they might return to the island, and there was a great oppression of the Britons and an overturning of the churches and a persecution of the saints.

WAS ARTHUR ORIGINALLY A GIANT?

Giants were common characters in British folklore. Geoffrey of Monmouth's *History of the Kings of Britain* described Albion (Britain) as a magical land inhabited by giants who continued to live there even after the arrival of the Britons.

Arthur's dog's name translates as "horse," his nephew Gwalchmai's grave was giant-sized, his companion Cai was known as "the tall," and Arthur is sometimes shown to be slow-witted, which is a trait often associated with folklore giants. Added to this, many geographical features across Britain are named after Arthur: Arthur's Oven, Arthur's Quoit, Arthur's Bed, Arthur's Seat, and so forth; all of these would best suit a giant-sized hero who perhaps shrank to a normal human size as part of a medieval reinvention.

THE HISTORICAL ARTHUR

Fragmentary historical sources and judicious deduction from folk tales have suggested that if Arthur was a genuine historical figure, he most probably lived in the fifth or sixth century CE. However, no reliable sources proving his existence have survived, and it is as easy to argue the case against an historical Arthur as it is to argue the case for him.

Despite the supposed years of Arthur's existence shown in *The Welsh Annals*, reliably dated references to him in literature and historical sources are hard to prove before the twelfth century. However, only a handful of personal names have survived from fifth- and sixth-century Britain, so this scanty reference should be considered preferable to no reference at all. Regardless of the scarcity of near-contemporary historical mentions of Arthur, a great

THE BATTLE OF BADON (NEXT PAGE)

This plate shows a fifth- or sixth- century British warlord and his warband riding into battle; many commentators have suggested that just such a warband was the catalyst for the legend of Arthur and his knights of the Round Table, but it also reflects our knowledge of historical Arthurian warfare.

The Welsh Annals tell us that around 518 CE Arthur won an important victory against the enemies of the Britons:

> The Battle of Badon, in which Arthur carried the
> cross of our lord Jesus Christ for three days and
> three nights on his shoulders, and the Britons
> were the victors.

This engagement is remembered as a siege, frequently envisaged as a British army from many kingdoms united under Arthur's command charging down from the ancient hillfort of Badon to decisively defeat the combined armies of the Saxon kingdoms. The sixth-century British historian Gildas mentions the Siege of Badon Hill, but does not connect Arthur's name to it.

British sources from the period demonstrate that some British warriors fought astride their sturdy native ponies, hurling javelins and following up with swords and spears, rather than riding enemies down with a lance in the fashion of a medieval knight. The poem *Y Gododdin* includes descriptions of British warriors on horseback:

> He cast his spears between two armies,
> A magnificent horseman before the Gododdin

> With shattered shield he tore through armies,
> His horses swift, racing forward

> He threw spears from the grasp of his hand
> From his steaming slender bay horse

many people have spent a great deal of time attempting to prove that a real Arthur lived, and they have built countless theories to support their ideas. No historian has yet presented a watertight case, but this chapter looks at some of the more popular theories.

The Fifth and Sixth Centuries

Few periods of British history have been more opportune for or better suited to a brave warrior hero than the fifth and sixth centuries CE: these were turbulent years of kingdom creation and incessant warfare.

The background to this Arthurian period is confusing at best, owing to the scant nature of the sources. Archaeology has provided some answers, and annals give an occasional glimpse into the past, but our understanding of the era's political history is mostly informed guesswork.

The fourth century CE saw the decline of Roman Britain, and between 407 and 410 Roman officials and armed forces left the island to govern itself and protect itself from neighbouring Picts from the north, Irish from the west, and Saxons from the continent. Some historians have argued for an ongoing central government – sometimes led by Arthur – although it seems more likely that the former Roman province fragmented into a series of small kingdoms little larger than modern British counties. British power started to give way to a Saxon elite in lowland areas during the fifth and sixth centuries; although often considered militarily weak, the post-Roman Britons resisted invaders for longer than many of their continental counterparts.

A few names of warlords and rulers have passed down to us from the immediate post-Roman period, and they have been drawn into Arthurian legend, but as with Arthur we cannot be certain if they were ever real people: Vortigern, Ambrosius Aurelianus, and the Saxon leaders Hengist and Horsa (who supposedly revolted against Vortigern in 449) all feature in both traditional histories and Arthurian legend.

By the mid-seventh century, the Saxons ruled much of the fertile English lowlands, forming a heptarchy of powerful kingdoms: Kent, Sussex, Mercia, Northumbria, East Anglia, Essex, and Wessex. British kings held power in the west of the island and some of the north, fighting against Pictish, Irish, and Saxon encroachment; Cornwall eventually fell under Saxon influence, and Strathclyde was finally absorbed into Scotland, but Wales remained a bastion of Celtic culture even after conquest by the English in the thirteenth century.

This helmet fragment from the seventh century Saxon royal burial at Sutton Hoo evocatively portrays warfare in the post-Roman period. A horseman with spear and shield rides down a sword armed, mail-armored enemy. (British Museum, London, UK / The Bridgeman Art Library)

Arthur the High King

The concept of Arthur as a high king – the supreme ruler above all other kings in Britain – ties in with the medieval interpretation of Arthur's reign as being over the whole island rather than over a smaller, regionalized kingdom. But it also draws some inspiration from the centuries of rule from Rome, when the land was governed as an imperial province, and from the period immediately after the collapse of Roman rule, when powerful warlords or civil leaders with military backing seem to have snatched power.

A possible, though seldom popular, solution to Arthur as a high king is that the early stories evolved from the life of one of Britain's self-appointed emperors in the late fourth century, and this is possibly where Geoffrey of Monmouth found inspiration for his stories. One of these British emperors, Magnus Maximus, had military success in continental campaigns between 383 and 388. He took with him a sizable army from Britain, and later featured as a figurehead in several British kingdoms' genealogies and as an important character in Celtic folk tales.

Stilicho, shown here with his family, was one of the later Roman Empire's most successful generals, and a real-life Arthur may have followed a similar career. (Basilica di San Giovanni Battista, Monza, Italy / Alinari / The Bridgeman Art Library)

Geoffrey Ashe's *The Discovery of King Arthur* (published in 1985) assumed that Geoffrey of Monmouth had recounted semi-factual history. Through ingenious detective work, Ashe proposed that the Arthur of Geoffrey of Monmouth's *The History of the Kings of Britain* could be identified as a British or Breton warlord named Riothamus. Ashe believed that Riothamus' name might have been a title rather than a personal name, translating as "Greatest King." His personal name, argued Ashe, could perhaps have been Arthur. Riothamus is mentioned briefly in contemporary sources as a Briton – probably a king – who crossed to mainland Europe and fought against the Visigoths in the Loire Valley. This happened in 468, and afterwards he was betrayed by the Prefect of Gaul and disappeared from history. It is possible that Riothamus was exiled to Britain at this time, as a result of the ongoing civil wars among the Britons in Brittany. He may later have returned to the continent, and perhaps died fighting Germanic (possibly Saxon) enemies around 470; he disappeared from the historical record near to Avallon in Burgundy, which gives Riothamus an obvious link to the legend of Arthur. Ashe saw Arthur as a *restitutor* – a restorer of the Roman way of life – whose real motives and deeds were distorted by

The Round Table in the Great Hall at Winchester. (Corbis Images)

medieval writers after Geoffrey of Monmouth touched upon his historical actions.

In *The Age of Arthur: A History of the British Isles from 350 to 650* (published in 1973) John Morris built his own interpretation of the period's history based around surviving sources and folk tales. Morris's Arthur succeeded Ambrosius as the supreme commander of the armies of the Britons, probably in the 470s and certainly by the 480s. Arthur managed to subdue Saxon encroachment across southern Britain, using cavalry armies, and fought the series of 12 battles immortalized in *The History of the Britons*, including the famous Battle of Badon in or around 495. Morris proposed that Badon was fought between Arthur and an alliance of Saxon kings including Cerdic, Oesc, and Aelle, and that this pivotal battle took place at Solsbury Hill overlooking Bath. Morris saw Badon as the final victory of the Britons, giving way to an era of peace during which Arthur rebuilt Britain as a post-imperial successor state, ruling as an emperor. Morris believed that 21 years after Badon, in or around 515, Arthur fell in battle against Medraut, a rebellious southern British chieftain. With Arthur dead, the short-lived revival of imperial rule ended, a revival more successful than anywhere else in Dark Ages Europe.

Leslie Alcock's *Arthur's Britain* (published in 1971) suggested a similar overview to Morris: that of Arthur as a major British warlord of the late fifth century who controlled large areas of Britain and fought against Saxons and Picts. Alcock firmly believed in the historical accuracy of the battles of Badon and Camlann, and dated them around 490 and 510 respectively. Much of the theory that Alcock proposed was based on early Welsh sources – in which he placed a high level of integrity – and he backed this up with archaeological research. Alcock's Arthur was cast in the role of high king or emperor in all but name: he had the military power to refortify hill forts across the south of modern England and to hold back Saxon advances from the eastern side of the island. Alcock believed that the real Arthur fought the 12 famous battles listed in *The History of the Britons*, as well as his final, unlisted battle at Camlann. Alcock placed Arthur's headquarters within the ramparts of South Cadbury hill fort, where he directed excavations in the 1960s. The sheer size of the fortification at South Cadbury suggests that the garrison was significantly larger than most individual kingdoms' armies during this period. South Cadbury had an earlier tradition linking it to Arthur, although there is nothing in Alcock's excavations to point to Arthur any more than to several other powerful military candidates who may have refortified the site.

The most straightforward proposal for Arthur as a high king is one that has been staring at historians since the mid-sixth century: was Arthur actually Gildas's Ambrosius Aurelianus by another name? Ambrosius Aurelianus was described in Gildas's *The Ruin of Britain* as the last of the Romans, and was possibly the victor at Badon … a battle inextricably linked to Arthur. The sidebar "Arthur the Bear" discusses the idea of "Arthur" as a battle name, and it is possible that Gildas's history instead used his personal name: Ambrosius. There are, as always, drawbacks to this theory, but it is one of the more persuasive arguments for identifying Arthur.

The concept of Arthur as a high king or emperor seems a sensible segue from the government in late Roman Britain to the kings of the Saxon era: some sources hint at the position of high king, and a role such as this would be possible in the post-Roman power vacuum. However, such theories tend to rely heavily on the few surviving written documents, which are not robust as evidence; is it better to ignore the scant evidence on the grounds that it cannot be proven, or build complex theories based on the information that has been passed down to us? The debate continues.

ARTHUR THE BEAR

A significant question remains unanswered in the search for an historical Arthur: if he was real, why can historians not find his name in royal genealogies or more frequently in historic annals? One popular theory is that Arthur was not the real name of the warlord, but a battle name.

Arthur was not a common British name, but the Latin word for bear is "ursus" and the Welsh word "arth." It has been suggested that combining the two as "Arthur" or "Arthursus" could bring political unity between Romanized Britons and their Celtic brethren, as well as conjuring up a ferocious image of the warlord in battle. When combined with the deeds of named historical figures such as Ambrosius Aurelianus or Riothamus, it becomes conceivable that Arthur could indeed have been the battle name of a leader we already know.

Another theory deduced from the similarity of the words "Arthur" and "bear" is that he originated as a bear-god named Artio or Artos, transforming from Indo-European myth to Celtic legend as a human warrior hero in pre- or post-Roman tales.

Arthur the Soldier

In *The History of the Britons*, Arthur is referred to by a Latin phrase: *dux bellorum* or "leader of battles." The most common depiction of Arthur in Celtic sources is as just such a warrior, possibly a protector rather than a monarch. Some early references even cite him simply as "Arthur the Soldier," and *The History of the Britons* noted that Arthur fought on the side of the British kings, rather than stating that he was a king himself.

Late Roman armies promoted good soldiers into positions of power, such as the Vandal Stilicho, whom Edward Gibbon remembered as "the last of the Roman generals"; could Arthur have been the Britons' own Stilicho? This has led to popular theories where Arthur held the late Roman military rank of *dux* (duke) or *comes* (count), and led a mobile field army rather like that of the later empire, consisting mostly of well-armoured cavalrymen. He inflicted a series of defeats against invading waves of barbaric Saxons in order to preserve the last remnants of Roman authority in Britain in the fifth century.

The statement in *The History of the Britons* that Arthur carried the image of the Virgin Mary on his shoulders or shield has led to a common generalization that Arthur waged a Christian war against his pagan Saxon foes. The history of the period is not actually so clear cut: Briton fought Briton, Saxon fought Saxon, and Saxon and Briton allied with each other when it best suited them rather than worrying about each other's religious practices. The idea of a war fought between the two cultures, between two religions, no longer stands up to scrutiny.

A more recent trend is to suggest that Arthur was not British at all. This is inspired by *The History of the Britons*'s hint that Arthur fought alongside the British kings rather than being of royal stock himself. Stuart Laycock suggested in his book *Warlords: The Struggle for Power in Post-Roman Britain* (published in 2009) that Arthur could have been a Saxon mercenary fighting for the Britons, continuing the late Roman tactic of fighting barbarian with barbarian. But more frequently Arthur has been linked to Sarmatian warriors from the eastern end of the Roman Empire. Sarmatian armoured horsemen were formidable opponents of Rome, and in 175 the empire recruited a large force of Sarmatian cavalrymen and sent them to Britain. We still have the name of the Roman general who commanded this formation of heavy cavalry: he was called Lucius Artorius Castus.

C. Scott Littleton and Linda A. Malcor's *From Scythia to Camelot* (published in 2000) proposed that Lucius Artorius Castus was the real Arthur of history, living a couple of hundred years earlier than anticipated. Despite the lack of firm evidence, Lucius Artorius Castus makes a fine circumstantial candidate as Arthur. Here was a man with a good military record, whose name and major life exploits were recorded on a memorial stone. He was active in the late second century as an officer in the Roman army, repelling raiders from the north of Roman Britain, and the list of

battles in *The History of the Britons* may have been based on his campaign. This proposed campaign was a series of running battles fought against an invading army of Picts, who struck south from modern Scotland to York across the Pennines, fighting battles on the rivers Ribble and Douglas in Lancashire. So although Lucius Artorius Castus lived long before the traditional dates given for Arthur, it is just possible that he became famed as a Roman warrior fighting for the Britons against their enemies.

Littleton and Malcor also suggested that both Arthurian and Holy Grail traditions derived from the folk tales of ancient Scythia; these stories were then carried to Britain by Sarmatian warriors serving Rome and became British tradition. Among the folklore of Scythia, the authors claimed, could be found stories of a dying warrior king whose sword is thrown back into the water; a magical Grail-like vessel; and a sword mounted in a stone. They went on to suggest that several characters from Arthurian legend might have been based on historical individuals who lived during the early years of the fifth century.

The suggestion of Arthur as a professional soldier rather than a king seems well balanced, but invariably leaves us no closer to identifying a good candidate. The Sarmatian connection is very appealing although Celtic tales of Arthur do not explicitly state that he was a cavalryman. The Sarmatian link becomes stronger only when combined with the anachronistic Knights of the Round Table. If Arthur was a soldier, he followed in the tradition of late Roman armies who employed generals based on their ability rather than their birthright.

Clive Owen played Arthur in Antoine Fuqua's *King Arthur*. This 2004 movie focussed on the theory that Arthur and his knights were Sarmatian warriors serving Rome. (Corbis Images)

Arthur of Wales

Wales was the final enclave of the Britons, who defended the hills and valleys against Saxon incursion. The British kingdoms of this region outlasted those of the south-west and the north; it was not until Edward I subjugated the natives in the late thirteenth century that Wales was really conquered. The pre-eminent kingdoms of Dark Ages Wales were Gwynedd in the north, Powys in mid-Wales, and Dyfed in south Wales. At various times, other smaller kingdoms existed, but these three were the most powerful and long-lived. Arthur was certainly remembered in the folk tales and literature of Wales, but no reliable evidence proves Arthur was an historical Welsh leader.

Gerald of Wales undertook a late twelfth-century journey around the Welsh countryside, recording the history, culture, and lore of the land. Among Gerald's recollections in the pages of *The Journey Through Wales* (*Itinerarium Cambriae*) and *The Description of Wales* (*Descriptio Cambriae*), Arthur's name appeared on several occasions. Gerald suggested that the famous early British historian Gildas never mentioned Arthur because the king killed Gildas's brother, and also gave an account of the discovery of Arthur's tomb at Glastonbury. Gerald named Glastonbury as Avalon, and said that Arthur's wounds were dressed there by a noblewoman named Morgan, a story that became well known in medieval legend. But Gerald also explained that the

THE STRIFE OF CAMLANN

The Strife (or Battle) of Camlann is recorded as an historical event in *The Welsh Annals* occurring in 539. The brief entry tells us that Arthur and Medraut both died there; later tradition remembered that Arthur and Mordred fought each other, Mordred as the usurper to Arthur's throne, and that after the battle the mortally wounded Arthur set sail to the magical Isle of Avalon for his injuries to be healed.

Medieval accounts of the battle depict a bloody affair ending with a final duel between Arthur and Mordred: as shown in this plate, Arthur impales Mordred on a spear but is struck down as Mordred pulls himself up the spear's shaft. In some literature, the role is reversed with Arthur heroically pulling himself along Mordred's spear. Arthur's loyal knight Bedivere watches the final duel, and it is he who returns Excalibur to the Lady of the Lake after the battle.

Of the battle, Alfred Lord Tennyson wrote in 'The Passing of Arthur' (published as part of his *Idylls of the King* cycle between 1856 and 1885):

For friend and foe were shadows in the mist,
And friend slew friend not knowing whom he slew;
And some had visions out of golden youth,
And some beheld the faces of old ghosts
Look in upon the battle; and in the mist
Was many a noble deed, many a base,
And chance and craft and strength in single fights,
And ever and anon with host to host
Shocks, and the splintering spear, the hard mail hewn,
Shield-breakings, and the clash of brands, the crash
Of battleaxes on shattered helms, and shrieks
After the Christ, of those who falling down
Looked up for heaven, and only saw the mist;
And shouts of heathen and the traitor knights,
Oaths, insult, filth, and monstrous blasphemies,
Sweat, writhings, anguish, labouring of the lungs
In that close mist, and cryings for the light,
Moans of the dying, and voices of the dead.

A reconstruction of the post-Roman fortress at Dinas Emrys in Gwynedd, Wales. Artwork by Peter Dennis. (Osprey Publishing)

Britons (perhaps meaning the Cornish or Bretons) "stupidly" continued to believe that Arthur was still alive.

That Arthur was a Welshman became a mainstay of many early theorists. Thomas Bulfinch wrote in *The Age of Chivalry* (published in 1858) that Arthur was a prince of the Silures, the Roman name for a British tribe in south Wales. Bulfinch placed the Arthur of history around the year 500, and raised him to Pendragon – a preeminent rank among the British nobles – about ten years after this. Sadly there is no solid evidence to support this popular idea.

In their book *King Arthur: The True Story* (published in 1993) Graham Phillips and Martin Keatman identified Arthur as a north Welsh leader who flourished between 490 and 520. His name was Owain Ddantgwyn. We know precious little about Owain, although Phillips and Keatman concluded that he fought against Saxon, Pictish, and Irish invaders and used the Roman city of Viroconium (Wroxeter) as his power base.

Steve Blake and Scott Lloyd put forward a novel argument in *The Keys to Avalon: The True Location of Arthur's Kingdom Revealed* (published in 2000). Concentrating on Welsh Arthurian sources, Blake and Lloyd attempted to reduce Arthur's geographical spread, suggesting that the majority of legends and early sources were connected solely with Wales. For example, they listed the Grail Castle of legend as Dinas Bran and the site of Arthur's court

Arthur and Merlin by Alan Lathwell. (Alan Lathwell)

of Kelliwick as Gelliwig. In a follow-up book, *Pendragon: The Definitive Account of the Origins of Arthur* (published in 2002), Blake and Lloyd pinpointed Arthur as a warlord associated with the north Welsh kingdom of Gwynedd. Blake and Lloyd, and Phillips and Keatman, both agree on the site of Arthur's last battle being at Camlan (with one "n"), close to Dolgellau in north Wales.

Chrétien de Troyes's medieval account of Arthur identified Montgomery Castle in Powys as the site of Camelot. Not far from Montgomery, near to Churchstoke in Shropshire, is the River Camlad. This is an alternative site for Arthur's famous final battle at Camlann, but as the river has been known by the names Camalet, Camlet, and Kemelet in the past, it is another possibility for the site of Arthur's court of Camelot, which neatly ties in with Chrétien de Troyes's assertion about nearby Montgomery. Both the Camlad and Montgomery are also situated close to the old Roman fort at Rhyd-y-Groes, which is one of the main locations featured in the Welsh tale *The Dream of Rhonabwy*. Sadly, there are no known suitable candidates as the historical Arthur from Powys, although Keatman and Phillips's suggested power base at Wroxeter sits within the kingdom.

One of the more obvious candidates for a Welsh Arthur, if based on name alone, has to be King Arthwyr of Dyfed (the principal Dark Ages kingdom

67

in south Wales). Arthwyr lived in the late sixth century – a little too late for the traditional Arthurian dates – but we know very little else about him. Perhaps Arthwyr's father, King Pedr ap Cyngar, named him after the great warlord, although whether Arthur was known as an historical or legendary leader at this early date we cannot be sure. It is possible that some of Arthwyr's now forgotten deeds were later drawn into the folk tales of Arthur, or that the king of legend is a composite of several such men. Baram Blackett and Alan Wilson subscribed to the theory that Arthur was not just one single, individual warrior in their book *The Holy Kingdom: The Quest for the Real King Arthur* (published in 1998). They proposed that the Arthur of folklore and legend derived from two real life men: Arthun (or Anwn), and Athrwys (or Arthwys), a king of the south Welsh kingdoms of Glywysing and Gwent. Chris Barber and David Pykitt's book *Journey to Avalon: The Final Discovery of King Arthur* (published in 1993) also identified Athrwys as the real Arthur, proposing that after fighting at the Battle of Camlann, Athrwys abdicated and travelled to Brittany, where he was remembered not as Arthur but as St Armel (or Arthmael), whose shrine may still be seen at St Armel-des-Boschaux.

There are many traditions that link Arthur with Wales, despite the lack of good historical data. Whether there is any truthful basis in these stories or whether as the Celtic language gradually receded into the hills and valleys of the west Arthur's geographical locale shifted with them, we cannot be sure. But local tradition takes many decades if not centuries to build, so perhaps there really is some truth in the idea of Arthur as a king in Wales.

A MEDIEVAL MYSTERY

Shortly before the English king Henry II died in 1189, an old man of British or Breton descent revealed to him the secret location of Arthur's grave: it was at Glastonbury Abbey. Henry's successor, Richard I, sponsored a search for the grave, and the Glastonbury monks dug it up in 1191. Within a coffin were held the bones of a huge man supposed to be Arthur, along with other smaller bones and a lock of golden hair from his wife Guinevere. An inscribed cross made everything clear for the excavators:

Here lies entombed King Arthur, with Guinevere his second wife, on the Isle of Avalon

Glastonbury Abbey had been devastated by fire in 1184, and funds were desperately needed for rebuilding; after the grave was found, a steady influx of Arthurian pilgrims arrived at the site and gave donations. Richard

I also had much to gain by showing that Arthur, the hero of his Welsh enemies, was actually dead rather than sleeping as described in Celtic legend, so would never return to help them against the English. Not only that, but showing Arthur to be buried at Glastonbury meant that the English could lay claim to the great king as one of their own heroes.

A drawing of the now lost cross, provided by William Camden in his 1607 edition of *Britannia*, suggests that the cross was actually older than the twelfth century, but was also probably not as early as the sixth century.

Almost certainly the revelations surrounding Arthur's grave at Glastonbury were no more than a tool of the propaganda machine used by the medieval English against their Celtic neighbours, located at a religious site ready to play along in order to rebuild its wealth and profile.

Arthur of the Southwest

Some early British folk tales about Arthur, and a growing number of post-medieval traditions, claim that he was from the southwest peninsula of Britain: Tintagel, Glastonbury, and South Cadbury are all sites that are now inextricably linked with the life of Arthur. Despite this, there are relatively few detailed modern theories regarding the historical existence of a southwestern Arthur.

In a world far removed from modern research, Arthur was linked to the southwest by many medieval writers. Geoffrey of Monmouth called Arthur the "Boar of Cornwall" and sited the Battle of Camlann near Camelford; he also noted Arthur's birthplace as Tintagel on the north Cornish coast. Gerald of Wales identified Glastonbury as the "Island of Apples" or Avalon, where the mortally wounded Arthur was taken after Camlann. Other medieval

Excavations at Tintagel uncovered a large quantity of North African and Mediterranean pottery dated to the Arthurian period. This suggests the site belonged to an important British leader, as shown in this 1994 English Heritage reconstruction by Ivan Lapper. (Corbis Images)

Arthurian stories are linked to the southwest, and the traditional site of Arthur's greatest victory at Badon is at Bath. In 1542, John Leland recorded that South Cadbury hill fort in Somerset was the real Camelot. Even the Welsh poem *The Dialogue of Arthur and the Eagle* refers to him as "Chief of the Battalions of Cornwall" rather than claiming him as warlord from Wales. We can no longer trace the validity of these tales, but at the very least Geoffrey of Monmouth, Gerald of Wales, and John Leland should be acknowledged as the godfathers of the southwest's modern tourism industry (alongside the inventor of cream teas).

Historians who favor a southwestern Arthur highlight the importance of the early British poem *Geraint son of Erbin. Geraint* is important as it immediately connects Arthur with the southwestern kingdom of Dumnonia in an historical context, rather than the usual tales of folklore and legend. It also shows him to be an influential warlord or emperor, whose men fought and died alongside those of Geraint at the Battle of Llongborth, but it does not tell us where Arthur was from.

A number of other Celtic stories make reference to Arthur as a great warlord or king of this area; the *Life of St Gildas* shows him commanding the armies of Cornwall and Devon in a siege of Glastonbury and other stories locate him within or passing through Cornwall.

Arthur's legendary court in early tales, Kelliwick, is traditionally sited at Killibury in Cornwall, and Arthur will forever be associated with the promontory fort and later religious center at Tintagel. The ongoing connection between Arthur and Tintagel was raised once again in 1998, when a team of archaeologists from Glasgow University found an inscribed slab bearing the name "Artognou, son of Coll." This stone can be securely dated to the fifth or sixth century, but although superficially similar, it is difficult to reconcile the name of Artognou with that of Arthur.

There is another theory linking Arthur to the southwest. Many traditional tales identify Arthur's grandfather as a Constantine, usually suggested to be Constantine III, an early fifth-century British usurper to the Roman Empire. But one early tradition remembers Arthur as the grandson of Constantine Corneu, a king of the powerful southwestern British kingdom of Dumnonia. Three kings of Dumnonia are sometimes said to have ruled at the time of Arthur: Constantine's son Erbin; Constantine's grandson Gereint; and Constantine's great grandson Cado. If this were the case Arthur would have been the son of Erbin, a prince and warlord but not a king.

The link between Arthur and the southwest of Britain is undeniable, but purely as a character of folklore. Very little historical fact underpins Arthur's connection to the region, and although it is not impossible that a real life Arthur ruled from the southwest, it is telling that the supporting evidence comes from legend and tradition rather than modern research or historical deduction.

Arthur of the North

Ranging across the north of modern England and much of modern lowland
Scotland, several British kingdoms fought against a tide of Pictish, Irish,
and Saxon invasions into their territories: an ideal backdrop for the great
warrior Arthur. Preeminent among the northern British kingdoms was
Rheged, which centered upon Hadrian's Wall. Other British kingdoms
included Elmet, based in modern Yorkshire, which fell to the Saxons at
a fairly early date; Strathclyde, which sat above Rheged with its capital
at Dumbarton, surviving to battle the Vikings; and Gododdin, a British
kingdom in southern Scotland which was immortalized in the poem *The
Gododdin* (which is perhaps the earliest source to mention Arthur, promoting
the argument for his northern provenance).

British history records the names of three northern leaders with names
similar to Arthur. A king named Arthwys ruled as a descendant of Coel Hen
(Old King Cole) in the Pennines, and the kingdom of Elmet had its own
Arthwys, son of King Masgwid Gloff. Little is known of either of these two
kings: certainly not enough to build a case for either of them having been "the"
Arthur. The third northern figure was Artúr, son of King Aedan of Dal Riada (a

kingdom of Irish settlers in modern southwest Scotland). Although probably born in the 550s and therefore perhaps a little too late for the traditional dates for Arthur, Artúr was proposed as a suitable candidate by Richard Barber in *The Figure of Arthur* (published in 1972), Simon Stirling in *The King Arthur Conspiracy* (published in 2012), and by David F. Carroll in *Arturius: A Quest for Camelot* (published in 1996). Despite Artúr's Irish origin, he is the first historically traceable "Arthur" in British history, so perhaps deserves more attention than he often receives. Artúr may have been based at Camelon in Stirlingshire, the name of which may later have corrupted into Camelot. We know little about the lives of these three would-be Arthurs, but it is tempting to speculate that some of their deeds may have passed into later folklore as aspects of a composite hero. Conversely, it may be possible that all three men were named in honour of a legendary or historical warrior hero who lived before or during their lifetime, in the hope that his prowess might be instilled in them.

Aside from Arthur himself, some other characters from Arthurian legend had their origins in the late sixth century and had strong connections with northern British kingdoms. The list is rather intriguing: Urien, a leading sixth-century king of the northern kingdom of Rheged, became the legendary Urien King of Gore; Owain, famous in later Arthurian legend as Yvain, was the son and successor of Urien and was celebrated for defeating the Saxons in the late sixth century; Arthur's sorcerer and advisor Merlin is sometimes claimed to have been based on the sixth century northern British bard Myrddin of Strathclyde, also remembered as "the Wild Man of the Woods," who went mad and fled to the woods of Caledonia after the Battle of Arderydd in 573; and Peredur, a British king of York who died in 580, became Perceval, one of the most famous of Arthur's knights. Perhaps these people were near contemporaries of a real-life Arthur, whose connection introduced them to later legend, or perhaps they were simply historical characters drawn into northern British tales of the legendary king.

It is not only personal names that link Arthur to northern Britain. In 2010 and 2011, the British newspaper *The Daily Telegraph* ran two stories with almost identical headlines claiming that archaeologists had found Arthur's Round Table … in completely different areas of northern Britain. One of these sites surveyed was in the grounds of Stirling Castle in Scotland; the other was a former Roman amphitheater site in Chester championed by Christopher Gidlow, the author of *Revealing King Arthur* (published in 2010). These theories stand or fall on the Round Table itself having been real rather than a medieval creation, and the table itself does not feature in any surviving early tales of Arthur.

A number of researchers have attempted to identify *The History of the Britons*'s list of Arthurian battles with sites in southern Scotland and northern England dating to the fifth or sixth centuries. Littleton and Malcor's theory

Voyage of Arthur and Morgan le Fay to the Isle of Avalon by Frank William Warwick Topham.

was outlined earlier in this chapter, and among the other theories are John Stuart Glennie's *Arthurian Localities* (published in 1869), W. F. Skene's *Arthur and the Britons in Wales and Scotland* (published in 1868), and more recently, Alistair Moffat's *Arthur and the Lost Kingdoms* (published in 1999). By analyzing the names of hills, rivers, and regions, all three managed to argue the case for suitable northern British sites for the 12 battles listed in the ninth-century account of Arthur's victories with some conviction.

The case for a northern Arthur is perhaps stronger than in other geographical areas, but the whole theory depends upon the likelihood of characters named in poems really being linked to a real-life Arthur, whether or not *The History of the Britons's* famous battle list remembered real encounters, whether Arthur really fought in these battles, and whether or not the authors who argue for these battles in the north correctly identified the battle sites so many centuries after they were first forgotten. If all of these questions can be answered positively, the case for a northern Arthur is promising.

The Case Against Arthur

There are almost as many theories about the historical Arthur as there are historians. This in itself reveals that the case remains open and most likely unsolvable. A broad consensus of opinion in the pro-historical Arthur camp agrees that he lived in the fifth or sixth centuries AD, and whether a king or not he was a successful warrior who fought for the Britons against the Saxons. Beyond these two points, little is agreed upon.

Set against this, the arguments opposing a real-life Arthur are persuasive. Thomas Green's *Concepts of Arthur* (published in 2007) judiciously argued for Arthur as a god turned folk hero. Most famously, David Dumville stated the case against an historical Arthur in the journal *History* (volume 62 issue 205, published in 1977):

> The fact of the matter is that there is no historical evidence about Arthur; we must reject him from our histories and, above all, from the titles of our books.

Despite Dumville's balanced and logical arguments, the quest for a real life Arthur continues unabated and his name still appears in the titles of books (including this one).

THE JOURNEY TO AVALON: WAS ARTHUR REAL?

Digging into the tales of Arthur, most readers feel the need at some point to decide whether or not he was real. Most of us quickly conclude that the medieval king of Camelot was an inspirational, fictional creation intended to demonstrate chivalric ideals.

But what of the more primitive Arthur featured in earlier tales? Arthur may be likened to a complex design of Celtic knot work: it is impossible to identify the start and end of the creation, or to decide what was pure legend and what may have a ring of historical truth. Helen Fulton, in *A Companion to Arthurian Literature* (published in 2009), described Arthur as a simulacrum: a copy with no original, because the surviving stories of Arthur always assumed the reader had knowledge of who he was; therefore we are never told where Arthur was from, what his role was, or when he lived.

Nowhere is Arthur's place in history confirmed and nowhere is it disproved.

GLOSSARY

Annals: A record of events usually arranged year by year.

Barbaric: Lacking control, unsophisticated, or wild; usually referring to people form another land.

Benevolent: Likely to do good deeds; kind.

Canonical: Part of a literary or creative group of works.

Chalice: A large goblet or cup, often for drinking wine.

Chivalry: The formal customs associated with medieval knighthood.

Confidant: A person who is trusted with keeping secrets or other private concerns.

Conflated: Fused or combined together.

Deposed: Removed from the throne or high office, often suddenly and with force.

Guise: An outward appearance or costume, often a disguise.

Heptarchy: An area governed or ruled by seven kingdoms.

Hilt: The handle of a sword or other weapon or tool.

Holy Grail: The cup or platter said to be used by Jesus.

Insubordinate: Rebellious or defiant of authority.

Medieval: Relating to the Middle Ages.

Otherworld: The afterlife or spiritual word after death.

Parley: A discussion or conference about an argument, usually between enemies.

Pedantically: Extremely focused on minor details.

Pestilence: Deadly widespread disease.

Piety: The state or characteristic of being devoted or religious.

Prose: A literary style that, unlike poetry, does not use regular rhythms and is more like ordinary written or spoken language.

Relic: An object from the past that is considered extra special because of its association with a holy person.

Scourge: Something that causes widespread suffering or punishment.

Segue: An interrupted transition from one phase to another.

Treason: The act of betraying someone's trust.

Tunic: A loose, knee-length (or longer) garment often worn with a belt.

Usurper: Someone who illegally takes power, possibly by force.

Dux Bellorum by Jose Daniel Cabrera Peña. (Osprey Publishing)

FOR MORE INFORMATION

Arthuriana: The Quarterly for the International Arthurian Society
North American Branch
English Department
Purdue University
500 Oval Drive
West Lafayette, IN 47907
Website: http://www.arthuriana.org
Arthuriana is the only academic journal in the world on the subject of Arthur and
endeavors to be a "multi-disciplinary journal of Arthurian Studies from
beginnings to the present."

The Camelot Project
University of Rochester
Rush Rhees Library
755 Library Road
Rochester, NY 14627
Website: http://d.lib.rochester.edu/camelot-project
The Camelot Project strives to provide a rich resource of Arthurian texts,
        illustrations, and other fundamental information.

Journal of the International Arthurian Society
Walter de Gruyter, Inc.
121 High Street, Third Floor
Boston, MA 02110
The Journal of the International Arthurian Society (JIAS) publishes all kinds
        of Arthurian literature articles that are based on literary sources.

Montgomery Castle
Castle Hill
Montgomery, Powys, Wales
SO 221 968
United Kingdom
Website: http://cadw.wales.gov.uk/daysout/montgomerycastle/?lang=en
This castle was Chrétien de Troyes's Camelot; although modern connections
        to the legend have faded, Arthur's Gate and Arthur's Street are still
        found in the town. Close by is the River Camlad and the Roman fort
        of Rhyd-y-Groes (which features in The Dream of Rhonabwy).

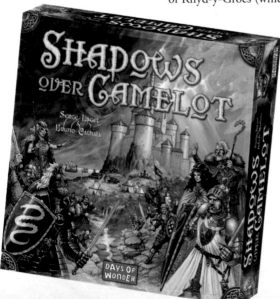

Tintagel Castle
Castle Road
Tintagel, Cornwall
PL34 0HE
United Kingdom
Website: http://www.tintagelcastle.co.uk
Geoffrey of Monmouth identified Tintagel
        as Arthur's birthplace. Today the ruins
        of a thirteenth-century castle occupy
        a dramatic cliff top site, and traces of
        an earlier Dark Ages settlement can be
        seen. Below the cliffs is Merlin's cave,
        and the village of Tintagel is a modern
        monument of Arthurian tourism.

The Great Hall
Castle Avenue
Winchester
Hampshire
SO23 8PJ
United Kingdom
Website: http://www3.hants.gov.uk/greathall.htm
The famous Round Table hangs in the Great Hall of the city that Sir Thomas
Malory identified as Camelot: it is a must-see for any Arthurian
enthusiast, even though it's no older than the thirteenth century.

WEBSITES

Because of the changing nature of Internet links, Rosen Publishing has
developed an online list of websites related to the subject of this book. This
site is updated regularly. Please use this link to access the list:

http://www.rosenlinks.com/HERO/Arth

FOR FURTHER READING

Alcock, Leslie, *Arthur's Britain* (Penguin, 1989) (revised edition)

Ardrey, Adam, *Finding Arthur: The True Origins of the Once and Future King* (Overlook Hardcover, 2013)

Armitage, Simon, *The Death of King Arthur* (Faber and Faber, 2007)

Ashley, Mike, *A Brief History of King Arthur* (Robinson, 2011)

Ashley, Mike, *King Arthur: The Man and the Legend Revealed* (Running Press, 2010)

Ashley, Mike, *The Mammoth Book of King Arthur* (Robinson, 2011)

Chant, Joy, *The High Kings* (Bantam, 1984)

Charles River Editors and Jesse Harasta, *King Arthur: The History and Folklore of the Arthurian Legend* (CreateSpace, 2013)

Coe, Jon B. and Simon Young, *The Celtic Sources for the Arthurian Legend* (Llanerch, 1995)

Cornwell, Bernard, The Warlord Chronicles: *The Winter King* (Michael Joseph, 1995); *Enemy of God* (Michael Joseph, 1996); *Excalibur* (Michael Joseph, 1997)

Duggan, Alfred, *Conscience of the King* (Ace, 1951)

Fulton, Helen (ed.), *A Companion to Arthurian Literature* (Wiley-Blackwell, 2009)

Geoffrey of Monmouth, *The History of the Kings of Britain* (Penguin, 1966) (translated by Lewis Thorpe)

Gidlow, Christopher, *The Reign of Arthur: From History to Legend* (The History Press, 2013)

Guest, Lady Charlotte, *The Mabinogion* (Oxford University Press, 2007) (translated by Sioned Davies)

Halsall, Guy, *Worlds of Arthur: Facts and Fictions of the Dark Ages* (Oxford University Press, 2013)

Hollick, Helen, Pendragon's Banner: *The Kingmaking* (William Heinemann, 1994); *Pendragon's Banner* (William Heinemann, 1995); *Shadow of the King* (William Heinemann, 1997)

Karr, Phyllis Ann, *The Arthurian Companion* (Chaosium, 2001) (second edition)

Lancelyn Green, Roger, *King Arthur and His Knights of the Round Table* (Puffin, 1953)

Lupack, Alan, *The Oxford Guide to Arthurian Literature* (Oxford University Press, 2005)

Malory, Sir Thomas, *Le Morte d'Arthur* (Signet Classics, 2010)

Matthews, John, *The Arthurian Tradition* (Aeon Books, 2011)

Matthews, John, *The Grail Tradition* (Aeon Books, 2011)

Matthews, John, *King Arthur: Dark Age Warrior and Mythic Hero* (Rosen Publishing, 2010)

Padel, O. J., *Arthur in Medieval Welsh Literature* (University of Wales Press, 2000)

Pryor, Francis, *Britain AD: A Quest for Arthur, England and the Anglo-Saxons* (Harper Perennial, 2009)

Stewart, Mary, *The Merlin Trilogy* (Harper Voyager, 1980)

Sutcliff, Rosemary, *Sword at Sunset* (The Book Club, 1963)

Twain, Mark, *A Connecticut Yankee in King Arthur's Court* (1889) (Penguin edition, 1971)

White, T. H., *The Once and Future King* (Putnam, 1958)

INDEX